PRAISE FOR *NO PLAN B*

'Many books are produced about the words and work of Jesus each year. Gareth's book joins this illustrious list focusing on the amazing Nazareth Manifesto. This book is insightful, challenging and encouraging. Get the book and be blessed by it. May it inspire you to engage with the Word and Spirit.' – **Colin Bennett,** Vice Principal, Moorlands College

'In over 30 years as a Christian I have never read an accessible book about Jesus' relationship with the Holy Spirit. Well, this is it! This is a book steeped in Scripture. Taking Jesus' message from Isaiah, quoted in Luke 4, as his jumping-off point, Gareth takes us on a challenging and provocative journey that leaves the reader crying out to God for more of the work of the Holy Spirit in our lives.' – **Marcus Honeysett,** Director, Living Leadership and Author

'*No Plan B* is a clear and accessible reminder of Jesus' missional priorities and our need to be empowered by the Holy Spirit in order to meet them. Not only would I encourage you to read it, why not buy a copy for a friend so that together we can fulfil God's purposes in our day and reach a lost and broken generation for Christ.' – **Adrian Birks,** Lead Elder, Honiton Community Church and Team Leader, Commission South West Hub

'It is quickly evident when reading this book that Gareth must carry the 'smell of the sheep' on him. He fearlessly addresses areas of common concern with a refreshing and keen intellectual insight without succumbing to overly academic language. I wholeheartedly endorse this book and would encourage as many as possible to read it.' – **David Campbell,** Regional Leader, Metropolitan East and West Regions, Elim Pentecostal Church

'A great book about how Jesus and the Holy Spirit worked together (and still do!), and what that means for you and me. Gareth is a great communicator and a clear writer: this book is well worth a read, not least because it is utterly encouraging!' – **Neil Townsend,** Senior Pastor of Wantage Community Church and Team Leader Open Gate Churches (Salt and Light)

'*No Plan B* is a timely book and rallying call for Christians to follow Jesus' example of ministering in the power of the Holy Spirit. Gareth has combined biblical exposition, personal experience and practical wisdom in this accessible yet challenging book. *No Plan B* is a must read for anyone who wants to "accomplish God's ends through God's means."' – **Dr Tim Tucker,** CEO The Message Trust South Africa and Author

NO PLAN B

NO PLAN B

A fresh look at Jesus' manifesto
and the mission of the church

GARETH LLOYD-JONES

First published in Great Britain in 2020 by The Message Trust
Lancaster House, Harper Road
Manchester, M22 4RG, UK

ISBN 978-1-9163489-0-5
eISBN 978-1-9163489-1-2

Cover design and typesetting: Hannah Beatrice Owens

To Sam and Sian,
with much love

'For I am convinced that neither death nor life, neither angels nor demons, neither the present nor the future, nor any powers, neither height nor depth, nor anything else in all creation, will be able to separate us from the love of God that is in Christ Jesus our Lord.' (Romans 8:28–29)

CONTENTS

FOREWORD

Having known Gareth Lloyd-Jones for a number of years now and having had the joy of working closely with him on a number of projects, I can tell you two things with absolute certainty. Firstly he is one of the good guys. With Gareth there is no public and private face; he is who he is and it's good stuff. I'm genuinely thankful to call him my friend but as well as being a good, old-fashioned, down-to-earth mate, he is also a man of God who hears the voice of God through the scriptures and unpacks it with humility, passion and power. This is exactly what you get in this book – real and relevant teaching that, in places, feels like it's dripping with anointing.

I'm so glad that we get the chance to revisit Jesus' manifesto for ministry in *No Plan B*. It really is as relevant and exciting as ever, and if more of God's people took it seriously and acted upon it I know the world we live in would be a much better place.

How much would you give to have been there on the day when Jesus came out of the desert in the power of the Spirit, took the scroll of the prophet Isaiah and read the words of chapter 61 with such authority that every eye was fastened on him?

His sermon on the back of that reading was only eight words long – 'Today this scripture is fulfilled in your hearing' – but the world has never been the same again. For three and a half years he lived those scriptures 'preaching good news to the poor, proclaiming freedom for the prisoners, opening the eyes of the blind, setting the oppressed free and announcing the year of the Lord's favour'. Then after the horrors of the cross and the glory of his resurrection, he gathered his disciples on a hillside and breathed on them saying, 'Receive my spirit. As my Father sent me, so I am sending you'. My theory is that Jesus was thinking back to that time when he was sent out of the desert in the power of the Spirit, where after wrestling with the devil for six weeks he received his mission and his calling. He was saying to his disciples, 'I've shown you what it's like to live out this good news; now by the power of my Spirit within you, you get to do that too'. So the amazing thing is that little, frail, insignificant you and I are anointed with that same Spirit within us to preach, bind up, release and lead just like the disciples were.

If Gareth's book in any way equips more believers to live up to that amazing calling the world won't know what's hit it. So, read on and feel free to get just a little excited!

Andy Hawthorne

INTRODUCTION

Virtually every time I watch Match of the Day, the same phrase is repeated. The losing team had *No Plan B*. I recently read the political obituary of a well-known leader and noticed the same criticism levelled at them. They had *No Plan B*. Football managers are applauded when they switch tactics mid-match and politicians are praised when they make pragmatic choices. Yet, God has *No Plan B*. Therefore, I don't believe he is looking for us to come up with a new, updated or upgraded mission statement. He simply wants us to understand and adopt his! For many years I have been captivated by what is popularly known as the Nazareth Manifesto (Luke 4:14–21). Some months ago I walked home having preached on this passage and sensed a frustration in my own heart. My problem wasn't with what I had said. It was with what I hadn't had the time to say. In that moment, the Lord settled in my heart the commitment to write this book. In doing so I trust that will help shed light on two things.

Firstly, the unique message this manifesto contains. As Jesus entered his hometown synagogue, he was handed the scroll of Isaiah the prophet from which he read a series of staggering promises. These were the promises of God concerning the coming Messiah. Jesus then addressed the stunned congregation by saying,

'Today this Scripture is fulfilled in your hearing' (Luke 4:21). Jesus came in order to bring: good news for the poor, freedom for prisoners, sight for the blind, release for the oppressed, and to inaugurate the year of the Lord's favour. As we take the time to examine each of these promises, we will discover how, through his life, death and resurrection, Jesus provided spiritual fulfilment to each of them. However, we will also see how this spiritual fulfilment leads to physical transformation. In doing so we will discover how social action, healing and deliverance should continue to follow the proclamation of the gospel.

Secondly, the way in which it helps to reveal Jesus' relationship with the Holy Spirit. Having explored this theme in the past, I was aware it was loaded with practical implications. If Jesus *did what he did and said what he said*, because he was God, then I was right to marvel. However, if Jesus *did what he did and said what he said* through the power of the Spirit, then I had some changes to make. God's plan and purpose is not that we rely upon our own resources, but that we follow Jesus' example and become dependent on the Spirit.

We will start by exploring Jesus' nature and seek to discover how he reveals his exemplary relationship with the Spirit. We will do this through an exploration of the Bible. It is my conviction that it is through the Bible that we start to get to know the Spirit. In the same way, it is only through the Spirit that we can really understand the Bible. The Word and the Spirit are not therefore mutually exclusive. Rather, each of them leads us to trust and to delight in the other!

Additionally, as we examine the mission of Jesus and his call to the church, I will prioritise Luke's gospel over the other three. Each of the gospels offers us a unique insight into the life of

INTRODUCTION

Jesus. However, it is only Luke, a medical doctor and travelling companion of Paul, who records the launch of Jesus' manifesto. As the only Gentile to author a gospel, Luke presents us with a unique portrait of Jesus as healer, teacher and Saviour of the world. As his gospel continues, Luke reveals the wonderful ways in which his manifesto is fulfilled. Luke's gospel is also distinctive in that it has a sequel. In the same way that his gospel allows us to understand Jesus as a man on a mission, so we will see in the book of Acts the church's continued commitment to further this mission.

Although there will be occasions when it will be necessary to explore substantial truths, I have sought not to deviate from the central theme. Therefore, for those who want to *dig deeper* or be directed to other resources, I have included substantial end-notes, which I trust will be helpful.

As we take the time to examine this challenging passage and its profound implications, I pray you will get a fresh glimpse of the glory and grace of Jesus. As we look at Jesus' relationship with the Holy Spirit, I trust also you will more fully understand, and then more powerfully experience, the Spirit's work in your own life and ministry.

CHAPTER ONE

THE LAUNCH

'He went to Nazareth, where he had been brought up, and on the Sabbath day he went into the synagogue, as was his custom. He stood up to read, and the scroll of the prophet Isaiah was handed to him. Unrolling it, he found the place where it is written' (Luke 4:16-17)

It was Steve Jobs who first launched Apple's iPhone to a media circus. Ever since, tech CEOs have followed suit. Having listened to similar presentations over the last few years, it appears that every new smartphone has more outrageous claims made about it than the last. It is said that each one will enhance our connectivity, improve our communication and radically transform our lives. But they don't. Well, at least not in the way that it was initially claimed. Ironically, in recent years, many of these *bright and shiny* launches have even been followed with the embarrassment of a product recall, as screens have shattered and systems failed. Of course this process is nothing new. For generations, politicians of all shades have gathered the world's press in order to present their latest manifestos. With confidence they tell their electorate what they will do if and when returned to power. They outline how people will be more prosperous, safer and healthier than they were before. Yet, as we know the delivery is often a long way short of the promise. I am sure that the vast majority of politicians have every intention to keep their commitments. However, once elected, they soon discover success takes more than good intentions. Therefore, despite being elected on a wave of optimism, it may be only a matter of months before the press and then the people turn against them.

With these two scenarios in mind, I want to turn your attention to a dusty synagogue in Nazareth and to events that took place two thousand years ago. The incident we will witness was without doubt the launch of the greatest manifesto of all time. It was not followed by a product recall, nor a failure to deliver. Yet, praise God, it is still being fulfilled... just as promised!

Luke informs us that after his baptism and the following forty days he spent in the wilderness:

> 'Jesus returned to Galilee in the power of the Spirit, and news about him spread through the whole countryside. He was teaching in their synagogues, and everyone praised him. He went to Nazareth, where he had been brought up, and on the Sabbath day he went into the synagogue, as was his custom.' (Luke 4:14–16)[1]

There is much debate as to the size of Nazareth in Jesus' lifetime. Although some claim it was a *one-horse town*, others believe it was a thriving hub with a few thousand inhabitants. One thing is sure: given the nature of Jewish culture, particularly at a time of oppression, Nazareth would have been a close-knit community.

Some years ago I was asked to speak at the church I had attended for the first few years of my life. As soon as I walked through the door, the sights and sounds seemed familiar, as did many of the faces. I suspect that the same was true for Jesus. Having attended the synagogue from childhood, this was home. He knew them and they knew him. They knew his mother, Mary. They knew his step-father, Joseph. Some would have recalled the scandal around his conception and the circumstances around *the* marriage. Some remembered his mum and dad travelling south in order to register for the census. Others may have heard the rumours about shepherds and wise men. All would be aware of the massacre which was intended to exterminate every baby boy in the vicinity of Bethlehem. Many more were present when the family returned home having first sought sanctuary in Egypt.

I am sure that among the worshippers there were many that had seen Jesus 'grow in wisdom and stature and in favour with God and all the people' (Luke 2:52). I guess too that a good number may have celebrated Jesus' bar-mitzvah at the age of thirteen. Some though may have only just moved into town and only knew him as the carpenter. I wonder if they even sat upon chairs that he had made. On this particular Sabbath, Jesus attended the synagogue *as usual*. However, in recent months much had changed. Jesus' fellow worshippers would have been well aware of these recent events.

- Jesus had been baptised by his cousin John in the Jordan River. They would have heard about, or possibly even witnessed, the conversation between the two and how a voice from heaven spoke and a dove had descended.[2]

- Jesus had gathered a band of disciples who followed his every move. Although this may seem a strange practice to us, the people would have been familiar with the idea of rabbi's receiving such commitment. However, I suspect that a carpenter had never received such devotion![3]
- Jesus had spared a bride's blushes at a nearby wedding, having *stepped in to save the day* when the wine ran out. Here Jesus had transformed bucket loads of water into award-winning wine. We are told, 'What Jesus did here in Cana of Galilee was the first of the signs through which he revealed his glory, and his disciples believed in him' (John 2:11).[4]
- Jesus had also performed a number of miracles, the details of which we are unaware. Later in the passage, Jesus suggests that the people will ask him to. He says, 'Surely you will quote this proverb to me: "Physician, heal yourself!" And you will tell me, "Do here in your home town what we have heard that you did in Capernaum."' (Luke 4:23). Although we do know that Jesus performed a number of miracles in Capernaum after this event, none are recorded before. It is possible that these are some of the miracles that John refers to when he writes: 'Jesus did many other things as well. If every one of them were written down, I suppose that even the whole world would not have room for the books that would be written' (John 21:25).

Given what they knew, I suspect that Jesus' very presence meant that there was a real sense of expectation. Should that not always be the case when we meet? Whenever believers gather, they do so in the assurance that Jesus has promised to be present.[5] And, whenever Jesus is present and acknowledged, then... stuff should happen!

It is probable that the synagogue was basic in structure and simply furnished. It is likely that the men would have sat on one side of the room and the women on the other.[6] The order of service would have been fairly straightforward. There was singing, praying and a number of readings, prior to the sermon being delivered and the final blessing being pronounced. So let's picture the scene, sense the drama and experience the emotion. Jesus is the local lad who has stepped into the limelight. On returning to his child-hood home, he is now given the honour of reading the scriptures. There is a possibility that Jesus had asked for the scroll of Isaiah the Prophet. However, the majority of commentators suggest that the synagogues would have followed a regular pattern of readings, in the same way many churches do today. Once the synagogue attendant handed Jesus the scroll, the sense of expectation would have risen. The tension, I suspect, would have been palpable. Jesus unrolled the scroll and found the familiar passage. Within the passage were words of promise that were filled with hope. Jesus read:

'The Spirit of the Lord is on me,
because he has anointed me
to proclaim good news to the poor.
He has sent me to proclaim freedom for the prisoners
and recovery of sight for the blind,
to set the oppressed free,
to proclaim the year of the Lord's favour'
(Luke 4:18–19).

I love the fact that Luke gives us such detail. I love that he informs us that Jesus rolled up the scroll, handed it back to the attendant and sat down. That's right, Jesus would have sat down and the people would have stood as he delivered his message. Then, as every eye was focused upon him, Jesus began to speak to them saying, 'Today this scripture is fulfilled in your hearing' (Luke 4:20). Later in the book we will look at how Jesus fulfilled these words through his ministry. We will also see how they remain at least a part of God's mandate for his church today. However, given that Jesus read these words from the book of the prophet Isaiah, it is really important to rewind the tape and look at the context in which they were originally written.

A BRIEF LOOK AT ISAIAH

Nearly eight hundred years before Jesus was born in Bethlehem, another baby was born not too many miles away. Like Jesus, his name was a prophetic statement concerning the message which he would deliver. His name was Isaiah, meaning *the salvation of God*.

It appears that Isaiah had significant access to the higher stratas of his society and therefore brought God's word to the power brokers of his day. Together, Isaiah and his wife, who was a prophetess,[7] faithfully ministered for around sixty years.[8] This ministry spanned the reign of four kings of Judah. Although we do not know for certain how Isaiah died, much Jewish tradition points to his brutal execution. The Talmud[9] suggests that he was placed in a hollow tree and sawn in half under the instruction of King Manasseh. There may be a reference to this Hebrews 11:37 which speaks about *giants of faith*. Although Isaiah is not mentioned by name, the writer does refer to those who died by stoning, were sawn in half or killed by the sword. I remember the first time I noticed that verse. I remember being shocked that this was the fate of some of those who lived by faith. For those who live in the West, it is essential that we remember our brothers and sisters elsewhere in the world who still worship and serve the Lord, despite many appalling threats to their own safety and security.

Although containing some narrative, the book of Isaiah consists mainly of prophecy. Indeed many of these prophecies are not even presented in chronological order. This means that even the brightest of scholars sometimes struggle to plot the timeline. As we look at Isaiah, or any other of the Old Testament prophets, it is important to understand their purpose and focus. Generally, these prophets spoke about the present, addressing themes such as repentance, righteousness and justice. These prophets also spoke about the future, speaking about what God would do in the years to come.

Isaiah spends a lot of time speaking about what is present. He rebukes the people for their rebellion. He speaks about their coming captivity and exile. He also speaks about their eventual return to the land that God had promised to them.[10] Isaiah even predicts the emergence of a Persian king called Cyrus, who would eventually defeat the Babylonians and allow God's people to return.[11] I want to assure you that detail like this isn't an unnecessary diversion. Rather, it is truth which has consequences for your life and mine. It means that God knows what we don't know. It means that God can do what we can't do. It means that God really is sovereign and rules over space and time. It means that somehow our God manages to fulfil his every promise and bring to completion his every purpose. Therefore you and I can rest assured in his promise that, 'we know that in all things God works for the good of those who love him, who have been called according to his purpose.' (Romans 8:28).

Isaiah also addresses what will take place in the distant future. The majority of people will have heard these words read at Christmas carol service: 'Therefore the LORD himself will give you a sign: the virgin will conceive and give birth to a son, and will call him Immanuel' (Isaiah 7:14). Sadly, only a few people know the importance of Isaiah 53 to Easter! Isaiah speaks more about the Messiah than any of the other prophets and for this (among other reasons) is quoted more often in the New Testament than all of the other prophets combined. Although in some ways we may see the Prophet Isaiah as the fulfilment of his own prophecy. That is, he is the one which God has anointed to proclaim good news to the poor,[12] but given the wider context it is obvious the passage is primarily speaking about the Messiah or Saviour who God had promised would come. In fact, so wonderful are the claims that Isaiah makes concerning the coming Messiah that in the fourth-century, the theologian and historian Jerome wrote, 'He should be called an evangelist rather than a prophet because he describes all the mysteries of Christ and the church so clearly that you would not think he is prophesying about what is to come, but rather composing a history of what has already happened.'[13]

By way of encouragement: it is always worthwhile, whenever the Old Testament is quoted in the New, to look at the context from which it is taken. In doing so, I am convinced that God will give you insights to thrill and inform you for many years to come.[14] However, if you do so on this occasion you will notice a number of differences between the texts that you read in Isaiah 61 and that which is quoted in Luke 4. Firstly, Luke's account has no record of Jesus saying that God had 'sent me to bind up the broken-hearted' (Isaiah 61:1). Secondly, Luke records Jesus as saying 'and recovery of sight to the blind' (Luke 4:18), despite us not reading these words in Isaiah. So what is the reason for these additions and subtractions? It is probable that Jesus was not reading from the Hebrew text that we translate our Bible's from today. Instead he would have most certainly read from a Greek translation known as the Septuagint.[15] That would at least account for *blind eyes seeing*.[16] But why does Luke not record Jesus *binding the broken hearted*? Was that not part of Jesus' mission and ministry? Of course it was and of course it still is! We need to remember that the gospel writers were in fact editors – each writer choosing specific things that Jesus did or said in order to present to us four distinct portraits of him. In fact Luke tells us in this passage that he doesn't share with us everything that Jesus said in the synagogue. He writes that Jesus, 'began by saying to them, "Today this scripture is fulfilled in your hearing"' (Luke 4:21). We cannot be certain as to how much Luke, under the inspiration of the Holy Spirit, has edited the account. But what is obvious is that he records Jesus as stopping at a very specific place. Isaiah initially says that the Messiah would 'proclaim the year of the LORD's favour and the day of vengeance of our God' (Isaiah 61:2). However, Jesus stops short of declaring God's *vengeance*. Why? Because that was not the main focus of Jesus' mission. Jesus came primarily to reveal God's favour and grace.

As we have seen, Isaiah was written at a particular time, in a particular place and for a particular reason. He spoke about God's people going into exile. He also spoke about their return to their homeland. But most excitingly, Isaiah spoke about the coming of the Messiah. Although Isaiah understood some astonishing things, we must remember, he didn't know all that we know. Isaiah no doubt assumed that the Messiah would come only once. We now know, however, that the Messiah has already come and will one day return. Between now and then, we continue to live in the 'year of his favour'. This is what is often called the 'gospel age'. A brief look at the text of Luke 4:18 helps us to understand exactly what this phrase means. The same Greek word is used in the passage on two occasions. On one occasion it is translated *freedom* for the prisoner and on the other *release* for the oppressed. Elsewhere it is commonly used to describe the forgiveness of sins.[17] Throughout the gospel accounts we see how Jesus places a priority on our spiritual state. However, as we will later see, the gospel so often brings with it physical manifestations and demonstrations of power.

BACK TO BASE

So let's come back to the Sabbath in question. Just for a moment, imagine the shock of those who listened. Make no mistake, Jesus wasn't predicting the imminent arrival of the Messiah. He was claiming to *be* the Messiah. Jesus, the local 'chippy', said he was the one for whom the people longed, yearned and prayed. It was he who had come to preach, heal and set people free, under the anointing of the Spirit.

In closing, let me share with you a brief story. Last year I was waiting for my wife in our town centre. It had been a beautiful day, but now, late in the afternoon, the sun was getting lower in the sky. I could see from a shadow that someone was about to emerge from around the corner. Yet the shadow gave me little indication of who it was. From the silhouette I could not be sure if it was a man or a woman, or whether they were young or old. Yet, as soon as they stepped into full view, I saw Tracey arriving in time for coffee. In many ways this is how the Old Testament reveals Jesus to us. It provides us with an outline of the Messiah, yet one from which we find it difficult to make out the detail. But as soon as Jesus steps into full view, all of the ancient prophecies become absolutely clear. We now see in technicolour what earlier appeared as only a shadow.

I therefore love the testimony at the beginning of John's gospel when we read, 'The Word became flesh and made his dwelling among us. We have seen his glory, the glory of the one and only Son, who came from the Father, full of grace and truth' (John 1:14). The Authorised Version, translated in 1611, uses a particularly lovely phrase. It records John as saying, 'we beheld his glory'. My prayer is that, as we look at the words and actions of Jesus, you and I would *behold his glory* in new and wonderful ways.

CHAPTER TWO

FIRM FOUNDATIONS

'In your relationships with one another, have the same
mindset as Christ Jesus: Who, being in very nature God,
did not consider equality with God something to be used
to his own advantage.' (Philippians 2:5-6)

A few months ago I spent a couple of hours at Dubai airport before
catching a connecting flight. As we took off, I could see the world's
highest skyscraper to my left. The Burj Khalifa was completed in
2010 and reaches a staggering 828 metres and 160 storeys high.
What I could not see were its foundations. Once I landed, a quick
internet search told me all I wanted to know. Before building up,
the construction workers had dug down. 194 reinforced concrete
piles, each 1.5 metres in diameter and 43 metres long, were driven
into the ground – each pile weighing in the region of 3000 tonnes.
I guess the lesson of the story is this: you can only build big build-
ings if you have good foundations!

The reason I share this information is simple. I am fearful of
building an argument on a flimsy foundation. If Jesus really did

minister in the power of the Spirit and calls us to do the same, then I want us to address a couple of *big* questions. Therefore, firstly, we will look at what the Bible teaches us about Jesus' nature. Secondly, in the next chapter, we will explore what the Bible teaches us about Jesus' relationship with the Spirit. Then, once we have dug down, we will be ready to build.

THE GOD WHO MAKES HIMSELF KNOWN

In the introduction to his brilliant book, *The Mission of God*, Christopher Wright recalls how, when he studied at Cambridge University, Theology and Mission seemed somehow disconnected. He writes, 'Theology was all about God – what God was like, what God had said and done, and what mostly dead people had speculated on all three. Mission was about us and what we have been doing.'[18] The problem is obvious. If we separate our understanding of God from our understanding of mission, we will end up with a wrong view of both. Any understanding of God that doesn't grasp his mission is flawed. Likewise, any view of mission that doesn't recognise its source is faulty. We must understand that God's mission doesn't originate in a synagogue in Nazareth, nor with Jesus' commission to his church. Rather, the mission of God flows out of the very heart of God!

Let me illustrate the point by reminding you of the words of David. David writes, 'The heavens declare the glory of God; the skies proclaim the work of his hands. Day after day they pour forth speech; night after night they reveal knowledge. They have no speech, they use no words; no sound is heard from them. Yet their voice goes out into all the earth, their words to the ends of the world' (Psalm 19:1–4). Isn't that wonderful? David understood that God had posted an evangelistic tract in the sky. That, from one generation to the next, the sun, the stars and endless galaxies would testify to God's creativity and power. In his letter to the Romans, Paul picks up this theme. Paul sees the heavens as a timeless signpost that point us to God's 'eternal power and divine nature' (Romans 1:20). All of creation points the same way. It was established in order that it would direct us to God.

We see this desire again expressed as God creates man and woman in his image.[19] He creates us, like him, to live in community, be creative and understand right from wrong. God created us for relationship with himself. Later, after *the fall* of humanity, God spoke to Abram and promised to make his descendants into a great nation. He later tells us that his purpose was, that Israel would be 'a light to the Gentiles' (Isaiah 49:6). Here, we see the heart of God again, to make himself known.

All of this of course brings us gloriously to Jesus.

The writer to the Hebrews opens his letter by saying, 'In the past God spoke to our ancestors through the prophets at many times and in various ways, but in these last days he has spoken to us by his Son' (Hebrews 1:1–2). Jesus then is the ultimate missionary on the greatest mission. His presence at the synagogue in Nazareth reveals to us the very heart of God. Greater than galaxies, clearer than humanity and more obvious than the Scriptures which speak of him; we see the glory of God in the 'face of Christ' (2 Corinthians 4:6).

NO PLAN B

THE MAN WHO WAS GOD

It is wonderful to note how through his birth, life, death, resurrection and ascension that Jesus fulfilled over three hundred Old Testament prophecies. I guess that God wanted us to be sure of the identity of the one who unrolled the scroll. So who exactly was this Jesus? To those who have been Christians for many years, this may sound like an obvious question. Yet, I believe that it is one which is essential to ask. For the first few hundred years of the church's existence, many of its leaders and theologians, fell out, excommunicated or even executed one another as they debated this question. It is my hope to avoid the former and certainly the latter! So here goes....

For time immemorial, people have wrestled with the meaning of life. Two thousand years ago, philosophers framed this discussion by using the term, 'the Word' or the *logos*. Some believed this to be a hidden truth, a particular idea, a creative life-force, or something yet to be revealed. However, John reveals the truth about the Word. He concludes that the Word 'became flesh'[20]. The question now had an answer. The Word was John's best friend, Jesus of Nazareth. So what brought John to such a conclusion? Firstly, he knew the Old Testament prophecies which he had observed Jesus fulfil. Secondly, he had watched what Jesus did and listened to what he said. On seven separate occasions, John records that Jesus uses the title, 'I AM'. To many of us this may not seem to be too important. However, to Jesus' first hearers it was shocking. 'I AM' was the name of God, which had been revealed to Moses as God talked to him through a burning bush.[21] On one occasion Jesus had told the crowd, 'Very truly I tell you, before Abraham was born, I am!' Immediately we discover: 'At this, they picked up stones to stone him' (John 8:58–59). On another occasion soon after, others said, 'We are not stoning you for any good work, but for blasphemy, because you, a mere man, claim to be God' (John 10:31–34).

Elsewhere in the gospels we find that Jesus regularly refers to himself as the Son of Man. Although this may not be a direct claim of his deity (his being God), it is interesting to note where we first hear this title. This designation is taken directly from the book of Daniel.[22] It is the name which is given to one who comes down from Heaven with power and glory. In using it, Jesus claims to be the one that is promised. Listen also to the claims which Jesus makes concerning that which the Son of Man would do. Here are just a handful from Luke's gospel. Jesus said, 'that the Son of Man has authority on earth to forgive sin' (Luke 5:24), 'that the Son of Man is Lord of the Sabbath' (Luke 6:5), that the Son of Man would 'return in his glory and in the glory of the Father and of the holy angels' (Luke 9:26), and that the Son of Man would come 'in a cloud with power and great glory' (Luke 21:27).

On other occasions Jesus also claimed that he was the Son of God.[23] Many others agreed with him, including an angel, the devil, the disciples, a number of demons, Nathanael, Simon Peter, the high priest, a centurion, John and the Apostle Paul.[24] Now in claiming to be the Son of God, some suggest that Jesus wasn't actually claiming to be God. Why? Because a son is distinct from a father. Or, because we as believers all become children of God.[25] Of course both of these observations are true. But Jesus wasn't claiming to be *a* son or a child of God. He was claiming to be *the* Son of God. An intrinsic part of the Trinity, consisting of Father, Son and Holy Spirit. This is why the writer to the Hebrews later shares these wonderful words, 'The Son is the radiance of God's glory and the exact representation of his being, sustaining all things by his powerful word' (Hebrews 1:3). That's right. The Son does not resemble his Father in the same way that I may have resembled mine. The Son is just like his Father in his very nature, being and purpose!

There are numerous other references to Jesus' deity in the Scriptures.[26] Although we have not got time to examine them here, there is one which will be helpful to briefly look at. In Philippians Chapter 2, the Apostle Paul is addressing his reader's selfish attitudes. As way of encouragement, Paul holds before them the example of Jesus. Through verses 6–11, probably a hymn of the early church, we are taken on an incredible journey. We begin with what is best described as the self-humiliation of Jesus and end with his glorious exaltation. These verses reveal how Jesus took the nature of a servant and became obedient to death. Even death on a barbaric Roman cross. We see in this moving passage how Jesus became a man, without ceasing to be God. How according to the Apostle Paul, he 'emptied himself'.[27] How, Jesus did not choose to use his divine privileges for his own advantage. Instead, he used those privileges for our advantage and for our salvation. Before moving on, I encourage you to stop, open your Bible and read the passage. Allow your heart to be stirred, your praise to rise, your attitudes to be challenged and your life to be transformed. Why? Because through the example of Jesus, God wants to transform us, just as much as he wanted to transform the Philippians.

THE GOD WHO WAS MAN

Having explored Jesus' divinity, we must also understand his humanity. Incidentally, over the years I have discovered that many non-Christians are happy to see Jesus as a man, but quickly reject him as God. I have also found many Christians who delight in his divinity, but struggle with his humanity. Although these believers seem comfortable with baby Jesus being nursed at Mary's breast, the idea that Jesus may have developed acne as a teenager is somehow viewed as blasphemous![28] However, for reasons that will become clear, it is vital that we grasp what John really meant when he wrote, 'The Word became flesh and blood, and moved into the neighbourhood' (John 1:14, The Message). It is essential that we understand Jesus' very real humanity.

Jesus was born of a Jewish woman in what was an occupied nation. He was born under *suspicious* circumstances and in relative poverty. Jesus spent formative years on the road as a refugee. He later became the big brother in a growing family. Jesus had an everyday name. It may have been loaded with prophetic promise, but I suspect he wasn't the only Jesus in the playground. Like other boys in the town, Jesus developed, physically, socially and spiritually. As an interesting aside, I sometimes wonder if Jesus may have struggled with his seven times tables. And if not, then why not? Jesus celebrated feasts, attended parties and interrupted funerals. There were times Jesus told jokes and times when he wept. Jesus had some close friends and others who viewed themselves as enemies. There were times when he experienced joy and other times when he expressed righteous anger. Jesus became tired, hungry and thirsty. Finally, Jesus suffered and died!

One of the most amazing passages concerning Jesus is found in Hebrews 4:15. Here the writer states, 'For we do not have a high priest who is unable to feel sympathy for our weaknesses, but we have one who has been tempted in every way, just as we are – yet was without sin' (Hebrews 4:15). Of course Jesus was never a woman, or old, nor encountered the traps of the internet. That means he didn't encounter temptations that may be specific to women, the old or internet users. So what does the writer mean when he suggests that Jesus was tempted in 'every way'? I believe that he is addressing general areas of temptation. If so, the passage must refer to temptations such as personal integrity, sexual purity and financial well-being. Therefore, we should be both humbled and grateful that Jesus was tempted, just like you and me, yet in every way and every area, overcame and remained without sin.

There is some discussion about whether Jesus had the capacity to sin. Some have argued that if Jesus could not sin, then the temptations referred to in Hebrews 4:15 were somehow less than real. Please imagine for a moment the final of an Olympic weightlifting competition. As the weights increase the contestants quickly fall away. Eventually we are left with two remaining athletes. The tension in the arena is palpable as the attendants increase the weight on the bar. The first lifter addresses the bar, braces himself and fails. Miserably. The second, however, with every muscle and sinew strained, lifts the bar high above his head. The crowd go wild as the champion takes the title. The point is this. It is only the one who overcomes who knows the full force of the weight. In the same way, it is only the one (in our case Jesus), who does not succumb to sin who knows the full force of temptation.[29] When looking at this subject, I'm aware that we find ourselves navigating a tension in our understanding. On the one hand, we know that

God cannot sin. Because, in being God, he does not and cannot change (theologians call this God's immutability).[30] On the other hand, we have Jesus, who took upon himself our humanity and yet did not sin. It is important to remember that the Bible often tells us what we need to know and not everything we want to know. It does not therefore tell us whether Jesus could have sinned or not. Although I may be persuaded by my friend Sam Storm's argument, I fully appreciate not everyone will be in agreement. Sam wrote, 'As a human, the possibility existed that he could have sinned, but by virtue of his unceasing reliance on the power of the Holy Spirit he did not sin. Like the first Adam, Jesus could have sinned. But as the second Adam, he chose not to.'[31]

SQUARING THE CIRCLE

Of course a circle cannot become a square and a square cannot become a circle. At least not without ceasing to be what they originally were. Squares and circles are different in every regard and are not therefore reconcilable or interchangeable. In the same way, some ask, how could Jesus be both God and man? Over the centuries some have argued that Jesus had a human body but a divine spirit. Others believed that Jesus flipped between man mode and God mode in the same way that Clark Kent may become Superman with a twirl in a phone box. Still others believed that Jesus was both God and man, but in reality, neither fully God, nor fully man. So, in AD 451, some of the brightest minds in the church hatched a plan. They gathered near Constantinople (modern Istanbul) and wrote a statement. They did so after much prayer, reflection and study of the Scriptures. I also suspect that they did so with the leading of the Holy Spirit. In their statement (known as the Chalcedonian Definition) they wrote: 'The Lord Jesus Christ is to us One and the same Son, the Self-same Perfect in Godhead, the Self-same Perfect in Manhood; truly God and truly Man... Two Natures unconfusedly, unchangeably, indivisibly, inseparably'. This statement has been held as a *touch-stone* of orthodoxy, accepted by both the Protestant and Roman Catholic Church ever since.

So there you have it. Jesus was 100% God and 100% man.

Finally, let's consider for a moment how all this happened. I am aware that any illustration is inadequate to describe the wonder of God becoming man. But, on the 27 August 1993, I became something I wasn't without ceasing to be who I was. No, it's not a complex riddle. I simply became a dad. I say simply, but there were many changes I had to make. Although I didn't cease to be who I was, I did not continue to live as I had. The theologian Millard J. Erickson said of Jesus: 'He is not some celestial superstar but one who has lived where we live. We can therefore look to him as a model of the Christian life. The biblical standards for human behaviour which seem to us to be so hard to attain, are seen in him to be within human possibility.'[32] This is essential. Why? Because, it means that Jesus came not only as our substitute in death, but as our example in life. As we will see when we explore Jesus' relationship with the Spirit, this is essential.

As I said earlier, this chapter was intended to provide a substantial foundation on which to build. But before moving on, I want to give you a brief encouragement. When our children were born, we immediately loved them on the basis that they were ours. Yet, as time moved and the more we got to know them, the more that love grew. When we first encounter Jesus, we love him because of what he has done for us. Yet, God's purpose is that this love should grow. So then, the more we discover about Jesus, the more we should love him, the more we should delight in him, the more we should worship him and the more willing we should be to serve him. That's why it's important to study and marvel at his two natures that lived and breathed and loved as one!

CHAPTER THREE

THE ANOINTED ONE

'The Spirit of the Lord is on me, because he has anointed
me' (Luke 4:18)

I had been a Christian for many years when I read a verse that
gripped me. In the book of Acts, Peter starts to explain why God
would do something as outrageous as pour out his Spirit upon
undeserving Gentiles. Then, bang in the middle of his report, he
says, 'God anointed Jesus of Nazareth with the Holy Spirit and
power.' He therefore 'went around doing good and healing all who
were under the power of the devil, because God was with him'
(Acts 10:38). Although that may not seem a shocking statement to
you, it did to me. Moreover, it captivated me and set me on a path
of discovery.

   If you were to ask a hundred Christians, 'how did Jesus do what
he did and say what he said?' I guess the vast majority may simply
answer, 'because he was God'. Of course they are right. As we have
seen, Jesus was, is and always will be God. Yet, Peter, an eyewit-
ness to so much of Jesus' ministry says in no uncertain terms,

that Jesus did what he did and said what he said because he was anointed by the Holy Spirit. Now, if Acts 10:38 stood in isolation it would be possible to overlook it or even interpret it differently. However, what Peter writes is repeated consistently in many other passages. So, in order to see how Jesus fulfilled the words of Isaiah 61, I want us to take a look at some of those other scriptures which speak about Jesus' relationship with the Spirit.[33]

THE SPIRIT AND JESUS' CONCEPTION

There was nothing supernatural about Jesus' birth. It was all very natural and probably very messy. The miracle of course was his conception. When mum-to-be Mary asked an angel how she could possibly fall pregnant, the response was straightforward. The angel told Mary 'The Holy Spirit will come on you, and the power of the Most High will overshadow you. So the holy one to be born will be called the Son of God' (Luke 1:35). A number of years ago I was speaking at our Christmas carol service. I explained how artists had tried to portray the wonder of the incarnation (God becoming flesh) for centuries. Having flashed a few examples on the screen, I assured the congregation that I would now show them the most accurate picture of all. I remember the audible gasp as I put on the screen a photograph of a baby, just eight weeks after conception. In the same way, I believe that we should gasp every time we remember that the Second Member of the Godhead became Jesus of Nazareth two thousand years ago. This astonishing truth should lead us to worship in the same way that it did Mary.[34]

Through the incarnation of Jesus, God achieved a number of things. Firstly, he revealed that salvation must come from God and not from humanity. Secondly, the means of Jesus' conception made possible that God could unite his deity and humanity in one person. Thirdly, the virgin birth means that God made it possible for Jesus not to inherit a sinful nature. Lastly, because of the sinless life that followed, Jesus was able to become our perfect substitute in death.

Lastly, we must remember that Jesus did not simply become a man for a brief window in eternity. Remarkably, Luke tells us in the book of Acts that when Jesus ascended (went back to heaven) his disciples strained their necks in order to see what was happening. The angels accompanying Jesus said, '"Men of Galilee," they said, "why do you stand here looking into the sky? This same Jesus, who has been taken from you into heaven, will come back in the same way you have seen him go into heaven"' (Acts 1:11). Did you notice that? We are not waiting for a Jesus who is somehow changed or transformed. But 'this same Jesus'. It is little wonder that the Apostle Paul tells his young friend, Timothy: 'there is one God and one mediator between God and mankind, the man Christ Jesus' (1 Timothy 2:5). Isn't that staggering? Today, a real man, really sits at the right hand of the majesty in heaven and really does mediate, pray and intercede for you and for me!

THE SPIRIT AND JESUS' DEVELOPMENT

The Prophet Isaiah had said of the Messiah: 'The Spirit of the Lord will rest on him — the Spirit of wisdom and of understanding, the Spirit of counsel and of might, the Spirit of the knowledge and fear of the Lord' (Isaiah 11:2). Although we know precious little about the early years of Jesus' life, there is one verse tucked away in Luke's gospel that we can easily overlook. Luke writes: 'And the child grew and became strong; he was filled with wisdom, and the grace of God was on him' (Luke 2:40). This short passage links Jesus to the prophet Isaiah. It informs us that Jesus' wisdom wasn't everyday wisdom, but Holy Spirit-given wisdom. It is interesting to note that the Greek doesn't suggest that Jesus would be filled once and for all. Rather, that he would be continually filled. If Jesus needed and received this filling, it is little wonder that Paul uses the same present continuous tense when he writes to his friends in Ephesus and says, 'be filled with the Spirit' (Ephesians 5:18).

The last thing we hear of Jesus' childhood is when he was aged twelve. Having lost him for a time, his mum and dad found him questioning the teachers in the temple at Jerusalem. Of course it would have been easy for those listening to look down on Jesus for his lack of formal education or indeed for his rural accent. However, Luke informs us that: 'Everyone who heard him was amazed at his understanding and his answers' (Luke 2:27). It seems obvious that Jesus continued to be filled with wisdom by the Spirit. It is little wonder that he grew 'in favour with God and man' (Luke 2:52).

THE SPIRIT AND JESUS' BAPTISM

Given that John's baptism was intended to demonstrate repentance, it is little wonder John took some persuading before agreeing to baptise Jesus. Of course, being perfect, it was evident that Jesus had nothing to repent of. Understandably, John argued that it would be better if Jesus baptised him.[35] However, his protests were in vain. Jesus was determined to be baptised by John. Even before Calvary, Jesus demonstrated his desire to identify with screwed-up and sinful people by being immersed in a mucky river. It is also possible that Jesus' baptism had an additional meaning. In the Old Testament there are times that priests who were about to begin public ministry would undergo a type of ceremonial baptism.[36] So then, even by the means of his own baptism Jesus gives us a glimpse of his *priestly* mission.

Luke tells us of the amazing events that happened immediately afterwards. He writes: 'And as he was praying, heaven was opened and the Holy Spirit descended on him in bodily form like a dove. And a voice came from heaven: "You are my Son, whom I love; with you I am well pleased"' (Luke 3:21–22). Here we witness a glorious glimpse of God the Father affirming God the Son. This has on occasion been likened to the inauguration of a president or the coronation of a monarch. It is a public affirmation of what has long been planned. But we also witness something else unfold. That is, the Holy Spirit, descending in bodily form upon Jesus. In doing so we see that he will empower Jesus in his earthly mission. Mark's record of this event is fascinating, suggesting that the Holy Spirit did not simply, come *upon* Jesus, but came *into* him.[37] Sam Storms suggests that this may be Mark's way of saying: 'the relationship is not one of mere external enablement but internal intimacy. Jesus was now the permanent bearer of the Spirit. Even if *filled* with the Spirit from Mary's womb, he now sustains a relationship to the Spirit unlike anything that has preceded.'[38] Isn't that an incredible thought? That Jesus grew in his experience of the Spirit from this moment on. If this was true for Jesus, I wonder: should it also be true for us?

Now, I don't know why the Spirit came from heaven in the form of a dove. Maybe it was because the Spirit is portrayed like a bird hovering over her nest in the account of creation. Maybe it was because a dove returned to the Ark with an olive leaf and in doing so told Noah that everything would be okay. Maybe it was because the poor were permitted to offer doves as sin offerings to God.[39] Or maybe, it was simply because, like the Spirit of God, doves are seen as gentle and pure. John offers a lovely insight into what happened at the Jordan River. He records John the Baptist testifying: 'I saw the Spirit come down from heaven as a dove and remain on him' (John 1:32). The word that John uses for 'rest' doesn't mean that the dove simply took a quick break. It means that it both 'rested' and 'remained'.

It seems blindingly obvious to me. If Jesus needed the anointing of the Spirit in order to minister in power, so do you and I. The idea that somehow we can do the work of God, in our own strength, with our own wisdom and leaning on our own experience is lunacy in the extreme. Remember, there is *No Plan B*. God intends that we fulfil his purposes, through his means. Therefore like Jesus we need a powerful encounter with the Holy Spirit. Like Jesus we need to ensure that we live lives that encourage the Holy Spirit to *rest* and *remain*.

THE SPIRIT WHO LED JESUS

I am sure that over the years we have all wanted to be led by the Spirit.[40] In principle it sounds really exciting doesn't it? In reality it is sometimes a little frightening. This is particularly true when we realise how the Spirit *led* Jesus. Prior to Jesus standing in the synagogue at Nazareth, we read: 'Jesus, full of the Holy Spirit, left the Jordan and was led by the Spirit into the wilderness' (Luke 4:1). The parallel passage in Mark is not quite so comforting. Mark says that the Spirit 'sent him out in the wilderness' (Mark 1:12). It is really important to discover that sometimes the Spirit leads us to places of abundance and sometimes he takes us to a wilderness. However, we must also learn that if we want to walk like Jesus walked, then we have to be willing to follow the Spirit, even if he leads us where we do not want to go!

THE SPIRIT WHO STRENGTHENED JESUS

There is no mention of the Holy Spirit's work in the life of Jesus during the forty days he spent being tempted by the devil in the wilderness. Jesus had been affirmed and enabled by the Spirit at his baptism, led by the Spirit in to the wilderness, and later, 'returned to Galilee, in the power of the Spirit' (Luke 4:14). But I find it impossible even to consider that the Spirit somehow abandoned him during his time of testing. Think for a moment at the way that Jesus, without so much as a bite to eat, was able to overcome the devil's schemes. He did so in a simple, but effective way. He quoted to the devil specific verses of Scripture, each taken from the book of Deuteronomy. That is brilliant. These words, spoken to God's people when they were in the wilderness, later become a strength for Jesus as he endured his own wilderness. In the same way, Jesus' example now provides strength for us.[41]

Lastly, notice again that when Jesus returned, he did so in *power*. I find it mind-blowing that Jesus wasn't weakened by this experience, but somehow strengthened by it. I am aware that none of us like to be tempted or tested. I am also aware that without these, we find no growth or maturity in God. I want to therefore encourage you. When you experience temptation, tough times, or wilderness experiences, allow the Spirit to strengthen you in the same way he did the Lord Jesus.

THE SPIRIT AND JESUS' MINISTRY

We will discover much more about this subject when we start to see in practical ways how Jesus fulfilled the promises of his manifesto. However, you may have noticed how most Bibles translate the phrase 'the Spirit of the LORD' in Luke 4:18. The capital letters show us that this verse, when originally penned in Hebrew, uses God's name Yahweh. So, whenever we read a capital LORD in our Bibles, we must remember that this isn't any lord that is being referred to. It is THE LORD![42]

Jesus' friends, family and fellow worshippers were all waiting for the Messiah. This term, used in The Old Testament in general as well as Isaiah specifically,[43] literally meant the 'anointed one'. (In the New Testament we find that the authors use the Greek equivalent which is Christ.) 'The LORD's anointed' had two possible meanings. It could refer to someone that God had chosen, such as a king, a priest or a prophet. It could also refer to someone who was divinely empowered. So which was true for Jesus? King David was one of Jesus' ancestors. The Prophet Samuel revealed that God had chosen him to succeed Saul. He therefore 'took the horn of oil and anointed him in the presence of his brothers, and from that day on the Spirit of the LORD came powerfully upon David' (1 Samuel 16:13). David was both chosen and empowered. The same of course was true of Jesus. This being both chosen and empowered is clearly seen throughout the gospels. Indeed his cousin, John the Baptist, testified about him that God would give him 'the Spirit without limit' (John 1:34).

In Luke we read three amazing passages: 'And the power of the Lord was with Jesus to heal those who were ill' (Luke 5:17), 'and the people all tried to touch him, because power was coming from him and healing them all' (Luke 6:19), 'when a woman who had been bleeding for twelve years touched the hem of his robe, Jesus said, "I know that power has gone out from me"' (Luke 8:46). I believe that it is highly likely that on all three occasions the word 'power' is a direct reference to the Holy Spirit. It was the Spirit who enabled Jesus to heal and the Spirit that both the people and Jesus knew flowed from him. Toward the end of his life on earth, Jesus said, 'I am going to send you what my Father has promised; but stay in the city until you have been clothed with power from on high' (Luke 24:49). There's that word again, 'power'. This promise, according to Luke in Acts 1:8, was fulfilled when the Holy Spirit was *poured* out on the disciples at Pentecost.[44] Throughout the gospel of Luke and the book of Acts we discover that the word used for power is synonymous with the work of the Spirit and the work of the Spirit is synonymous with power.

Now as we will see, Jesus didn't just heal and perform in the power of the Spirit, he also taught in the power of the Spirit. In fact Luke even opens the book of Acts by saying that in his earlier gospel he had written: 'about all that Jesus began to do and to teach until the day he was taken up to heaven, after giving instructions through the Holy Spirit to the apostles he had chosen' (Acts 1:2). The instructions that Jesus gave to his disciples were, according to Luke, given through the Spirit every bit as much as the miracles he performed.

Lastly, if you have been a Christian for any length of time, you will have asked or been asked what Jesus meant when he spoke about blasphemy of the Spirit. Like me I suspect that in the past you may have missed the wood for the trees! In short, Jesus healed a man who is both blind and mute. Rather than rejoicing, Jesus' enemies accused him of driving out demons by the power of Satan. Jesus answers them by saying: 'I tell you, every kind of sin and slander can be forgiven, but blasphemy against the Spirit will not be forgiven' (Matthew 12:31). Notice, Jesus is the first person to make mention of the Holy Spirit in the conversation. Why? I believe that the answer is obvious. Jesus is revealing that *he did what he did and said what he said, by the power of the Spirit.*

THE SPIRIT WHO BROUGHT JESUS JOY

The prophet Isaiah says about the coming Messiah that he would be: 'despised and rejected by mankind, a man of suffering, and familiar with pain. Like one from whom people hide their faces he was despised, and we held him in low esteem' (Isaiah 53:3). That description is of course true of Jesus. However, Luke also gives us another insight into Jesus after he commissioned his disciples to make known the good news of the kingdom. Luke's record tells us that Jesus didn't just send out the twelve, he sent out the seventy-two. When they returned Luke says that Jesus was 'full of joy through the Holy Spirit' (Luke 10:21). That's fabulous! Jesus may have been a man who suffered greatly, but he also knew great joy. In light of that, I want to assure you that he still celebrates when you or I are willing to act in obedience. Jesus is still filled with joy when his power is revealed in our weakness.[45]

THE SPIRIT WHO HELPED JESUS IN DEATH

John the Baptist had said of Jesus that God would give him 'the Spirit without limit' (John 3:34). As we have seen, this was very much true of Jesus' life and ministry. It was also true of his death. Although the writer to the Hebrews opens his letter with a breathtaking portrait of the divinity of Jesus, he also takes time to assure us of his real humanity. It should be no shock then that the Spirit who led Jesus into the wilderness would help to strengthen and sustain him on the road to Calvary. In Hebrews 9:14 we then read these amazing words that Jesus, 'through the eternal Spirit offered himself unblemished to God.' By strengthening Jesus throughout his life, the Spirit helped to ensure that Jesus was able to offer himself upon the cross as a perfect sacrifice for sin.

Isn't it comforting that the Spirit does not only help in the good times? God not only grants us his Holy Spirit that we can live well, but also that we may die well!

THE SPIRIT AND JESUS' RESURRECTION

The temple in Jerusalem was breathtaking. Having taken forty-six years to build, it was the pride of the nation. One day Jesus stood in its impressive courts and said, 'Destroy this temple, and I will raise it again in three days' (John 2:19). The people were outraged, but John goes on to tell us that Jesus wasn't speaking about its bricks and mortar. Jesus was speaking about himself! It was through him and not this building that people could enter a real relationship with almighty God. In Acts Chapter 10, Peter gives us another take on this truth. In one of the most important sermons in the whole Bible, he tells the first non-Jewish converts what exactly had happened to Jesus. He says, 'We are witnesses of everything he did in the country of the Jews and in Jerusalem. They killed him by hanging him on a cross, but God raised him from the dead on the third day and caused him to be seen' (Acts 10:39–40). Having heard firstly, that Jesus was responsible for his own resurrection and secondly, that God himself claimed to be behind it, we now turn our attention to Romans 8:11. Here Paul says, 'And if the Spirit of him who raised Jesus from the dead is living in you, he who raised Christ from the dead will also give life to your mortal bodies because of his Spirit who lives in you.'

It would of course be ridiculous to imagine that there is any contradiction between these three statements. Instead we again see God the Father, God the Son and God the Holy Spirit, working in unity and harmony. The Trinity works as one in order to execute the plan that had been devised in eternity past. Can it get any better than this? It does! Paul says that we also receive this same Spirit in order that we may also receive resurrection life. Not a Spirit which is lesser, weaker or in any way diluted, but the same Holy Spirit that raised our Lord Jesus. [46]

THE ANOINTED ONE

THE SPIRIT AND JESUS' ONGOING MINISTRY THROUGH US

Again, more about this later. But just to whet your appetite....

John the Baptist said about Jesus, 'I saw the Spirit come down from heaven as a dove and remain on him. And I myself did not know him, but the one who sent me to baptise with water told me, "The man on whom you see the Spirit come down and remain is the one who will baptise with the Holy Spirit."' (John 1:32–33). At the beginning of Jesus' public ministry, John received revelation concerning the future. He knew that he could only *dunk* people in water as an act of repentance, but Jesus would see them saturated in the Spirit.

Through the ministry of Jesus we see this promise start to be fulfilled through the ministry of his disciples. However, while preparing them for his departure, Jesus said to his followers, 'And I will ask the Father, and he will give you another advocate to help you and be with you for ever – the Spirit of truth' (John 14:16–17). Although Jesus wouldn't be physically present forever, his Spirit would. Then again, after his resurrection, John records that Jesus 'breathed on them and said, "Receive the Holy Spirit"' (Acts 20:22). In every way this seems to foreshadow the incredible coming of the Spirit on the Day of Pentecost, recorded in Acts Chapter 2.

Having shared a number of passages, I want to make one thing absolutely clear. The relationship that Jesus had with the Holy Spirit wasn't simply functional or practical. It was intimate and personal. In the same way when we read Jesus' promises to us concerning his Spirit we need to remember: God doesn't give us fuel, or a force, or an inanimate power to do his work. God gives us himself! Isn't that breathtaking?[47]

SPEECHLESS

I want to tell you a brief story in order to put this chapter in a right and proper perspective. One Sunday morning I plucked up the courage to speak about the Trinity at the church I pastored. I remember walking home with our son who was then just a teenager. Sam said something that shocked me. He said, 'that was brilliant this morning, Dad'. I was almost speechless! In shock I managed to find the words and ask the question, 'why?' Sam's reply was better than I could have imagined. He said, 'because you don't really understand it, do you?' He was right, I didn't then and I don't now! A couple of months later I was comforted by some words that I read. Although I cannot recall the author, I do remember their impact. The writer said something along the lines of, 'it is not my job to fully explain God, but only to describe what I see in Scripture'. Now, I don't fully understand the universe, but I marvel at it. I have little idea how the food I eat is turned into energy, but I am thankful for it. I have little insight into what goes on inside my laptop, but have come to rely upon it. In the same way, I would be a fool to believe that I can fully understand or indeed explain everything about God's triune nature. I do however pray that this chapter will have encouraged you to delight in him as we have spent time exploring the Bible together.[48]

CHAPTER FOUR

PREACH

'Because he has anointed me to proclaim good news'
(Luke 4:18)

It was August 31 2008 and the last day of the summer football transfer window. I went to bed about 11pm thinking that there would be no more *comings or goings* at Manchester City. Suddenly, just before midnight, our son crashed into our room. In sheer delight, Sam in breathless excitement announced, 'Dad, we've bought Robinho.' This wasn't any news, this was great news. I clearly remember my reaction. I couldn't have leapt out of bed quicker if I had been told the house was alight. We both tumbled down the stairs and booted up the computer. We found our way to YouTube and sat mesmerised as we watched the Brazilian's tricks and flicks. That may seem ridiculous to some, particularly those who remember Robinho! Yet, to a football-daft young lad (and his equally ridiculous father), this was *good news that brought great joy!*

I am sure that we can all think of announcements that we would love to hear. What about calorie-free cakes, the reversal of global warming or even a universal cure for cancer? I assure you, the announcement Jesus made at the synagogue in Nazareth was greater than any of these. It was greater than any that had been made before and greater than any made after. However I am sure that if you commissioned a questionnaire and asked people, 'what was so great about this announcement?' not many people would put preaching at the top of their list. Why? Because preaching is old school, irrelevant, out-dated, out-moded, autocratic, patronising, monotonous or just downright boring. Really? Well I guess it all depends on who is preaching and what is being preached! Jesus took the scroll and read, 'The Spirit of the Lord is on me, because he has anointed me to proclaim good news to the poor' (Luke 4:18).

I am told that Inuit have around fifty words for snow and know that ancient Greek had around a dozen for preaching. These Greek words are not interchangeable. They were not different ways of saying the same thing. Each word has its own specific meaning in order to describe exactly what is taking place. When scholars gathered to translate Isaiah (originally written in Hebrew) into Greek (the primary written language of the New Testament era), they chose their words carefully. When wanting to describe what the Spirit would empower the Messiah to do, the word they chose was *euangelasathai*. This literally means to *proclaim good news that brings great joy*. As a verb it is used over fifty times in the New Testament. Yet other words derived from the same root are used more frequently. We translate these as evangelist, evangelical, evangelisation and evangel.

In order to appreciate the intent of these scholars, it is important to understand how this word would have been used in a historical context. Imagine then, an ancient society where the men of the region have formed an army in order to fight off an aggressor. Day after day, the women, children and those men too old or infirmed to fight wait for news. They know that bad news will mean their fathers and sons have died. Bad news may also mean that they will be slaughtered or taken as slaves. Then suddenly, there is a cloud of dust on the horizon. A messenger emerges on horseback. Even before the horse stops, people are running from every direction in order to hear the news. The announcement is simple. Victory. The enemy has been defeated and their army has overcome. The evangelist proclaims the evangel. Or, as it is translated in our Bibles, the *gospel.*

WHAT NEWS?

How does the Bible define the gospel, or the *good news that brings great joy*? I have chosen a number of passages that speak about the preaching of the gospel. The passages are not exhaustive, but are chosen to be representative, in order to give an overview. Let's start with the gospel of Luke.

The word *euangelasathai* is used by Luke even before Jesus is born. As Zechariah served in the temple, an angel appeared to the ageing priest. The angel said, 'I am Gabriel. I stand in the presence of God, and I have been sent to speak to you and to tell you this good news' (Luke 1:19). The news concerned the birth of Zechariah's son John, who later became known as 'the Baptist'. Then, immediately after the birth of Jesus, the angel spoke again.

45

This time to shepherds. Understandably the shepherds were terrified as one angel was joined by a host of others. But the angel assured them saying, 'Do not be afraid. I bring you good news that will cause great joy for all the people. Today in the town of David a Saviour has been born to you; he is the Messiah, the Lord' (Luke 2:10–11). Although these two occasions help our understanding that the gospel should be proclaimed or announced, they don't fully clarify what the gospel is.

So let's look at Jesus' ministry. Immediately after he left the synagogue in Nazareth, Jesus headed for the nearby town of Capernaum. Here we see a series of snapshots of Jesus *in action*. A demonised man is delivered, Simon's mother-in-law is cured of a high fever and some are healed and others freed from demons. Unsurprisingly, the people asked Jesus to stay, yet his response was simple. Jesus said, 'I must proclaim the good news of the kingdom of God to the other towns also, because that is why I was sent' (Luke 4:43). Don't get me wrong. Jesus' healing and deliverance was not only important, it was essential. Although the crowds appreciated the *signs and wonders* it is obvious that Jesus knew the priority of his mission. It was to *bring good news that would bring great joy*. Jesus called it the gospel of the kingdom. This is a term he uses again in Luke 8:1 and then in Luke 16:6. We know that the Jewish people were oppressed and downtrodden by the Romans. They were riddled with in fighting and division. The only thing that appeared to unite them was their longing for the Messiah to come and to restore the kingdom of Israel. By announcing himself as Messiah, Jesus proclaimed that the kingdom was no longer a future hope, but rather a present reality!

So what was the nature of this kingdom? The people were looking for a physical kingdom along with the restoration of political power. In short, the people wanted their land back. However, Jesus offered them something very different. The kingdom that he brought was not physical, but spiritual. On one occasion Jesus said, 'if I drive out demons by the finger of God, then the kingdom of God has come upon you' (Luke 1:20). Did you grasp that? Jesus didn't drive out the Romans, he dealt with the occupation of demons! This distinction between the people's expectation and Jesus' message can be seen throughout his ministry. It is seen both in his dealings with the people and with his own disciples. In Acts, Luke records the moments before Jesus returned to heaven. The disciples gathered around and asked, 'Lord, are you at this time going to restore the kingdom to Israel?' But Jesus said to them, 'It is not for you to know the times or dates the Father has set by his own authority. But you will receive power when the Holy Spirit comes on you; and you will be my witnesses in Jerusalem, and in all Judea and Samaria, and to the ends of the earth' (Luke 1:7–8). Again we see the disciples are concerned with the imminent future of the Jewish nation. However, Jesus is primarily concerned with the eternal destiny of the *ends of the earth.*

In many ways these truths should have already been grasped by the disciples. Jesus had given them 'power and authority to drive out all demons and to cure diseases'. Furthermore, 'he sent them out to proclaim the Kingdom of God and to heal those who were ill' (Luke 9:1–2). This short passage shows us that Jesus was now not doing all of the preaching. The disciples were also preaching about Jesus! They were proclaiming *good news that brings great joy.* Nor was it Jesus who was doing all the healing and deliverance. The disciples were now moving in the supernatural, in Jesus' name.

In the book of Acts, the Apostles continue to proclaim the
gospel of the kingdom. We see in Acts 13, Paul and his team arrive
at Pisidian Antioch. On the Sabbath day they attended a synagogue. After the reading of the Law and the Prophets, they were
offered the opportunity to speak. Paul took the chance to address
the worshippers, providing them with a whistle-stop tour of God's
dealings and promises to Israel. It is little surprise then, that in
verse 32 he says, 'We tell you the good news: what God promised
our ancestors he has fulfilled for us, their children, by raising up
Jesus. As it is written in the second Psalm: "You are my son; today
I have become your father"' (Acts 13:32). Again it is easy to miss
the significance of this and similar statements. Paul is proclaiming
the *good news that brings great joy*. God's kingdom had come.
Why? Because Jesus the Messiah had conquered the grave. Without
this victory, there would be no triumph, no kingdom and no good
news.

Lastly, we come to the New Testament letters where we discover
that the writers continue to encourage their readers with the
gospel. Paul goes so far as to say that the gospel is important that
'even if we or an angel from heaven should preach a gospel other
than the one we preached to you, let them be under God's curse!'
(Galatians 1:8). That's some statement. But, according to Paul, the
gospel is not a matter of opinion, a piece of helpful advice, nor a
life-style option. The gospel is a life or death reality!

PREACH

A DEFINING QUESTION

So let's ask again. Exactly what is the gospel?

A few weeks ago I listened to my good friend Peter Cockrell teaching a group of ministry trainees. He wanted them to understand that not everything we believe about our faith is of equal importance. To prove his point, Pete shared a challenge that he had given to pastors in East Africa. The challenge was this: 'Imagine you have travelled home and it was now late in the day. As you turn the corner of your street you see that your home is on fire. You have a few short moments in order to save some of your possessions. What do you save?' The answer that the trainees gave revealed what they valued the most. It was a recognition that not everything that they possessed was of equal importance. We then came back to the question of the day: 'Which truths concerning Jesus do you value the most?'

If we had the opportunity to present this challenge to the Apostle Paul, I think we can be pretty sure of the answer he would give. Paul writes:

'Now, brothers and sisters, I want to remind you of the gospel I preached to you, which you received and on which you have taken your stand. By this gospel you are saved, if you hold firmly to the word I preached to you. Otherwise, you have believed in vain. For what I received I passed on to you as of first importance: that Christ died for our sins according to the Scriptures, that he was buried, that he was raised on the third day according to the Scriptures, and that he appeared to Cephas, and then to the Twelve. After that, he appeared to more than five hundred of the brothers and sisters at the same time, most of whom are still living, though some have fallen asleep. Then he appeared to James, then to all the apostles, and last of all he appeared to me also, as to one abnormally born' (1 Corinthians 15:1–8).

According to Paul he valued the gospel, referring to it as 'of first importance'. Paul defines this gospel as a series of events. He mentions four things:

- That this series of events took place according to the Scriptures. The gospel didn't *just happen*, it was planned and foretold by God.
- The Christ, God's anointed, died in our place and for our sin.
- That Christ was buried. This is often overlooked, but I have witnessed how, at burials or cremations, people often start to speak of the deceased in the past tense. A person's burial is often perceived as the place of no return.
- That on the third day Christ was raised. He was then seen by over five hundred people, many of whom were still alive.

THE DEFINITION

In recent years there has been a great deal of discussion about how we should describe or define the gospel. Books have been written, conferences held and symposiums gathered. However, much disagreement still remains. Although there are a numerous reasons why, one thing strikes me forcibly. That is, different people seem to focus exclusively on different parts of the Bible in order to define the 'gospel'. On one side, there are those who live in the Old Testament and seldom venture into the New. Then there are others, who believe Jesus' words to be primary and everything else subsidiary. However, I am convinced that if we are to fully understand the gospel, we need to use every piece of the jigsaw which God has given us. This is what Paul calls 'the whole counsel of God' (Acts 20:27). This means:

- We must honour the Old Testament, remembering that Jesus claimed to be a fulfilment of all that was written in the 'Law of Moses, the Prophets and the Psalms' (Luke 24:44).   ˙
- We should understand the value of Jesus' life, as the promised Messiah; his death, where he provided the penalty for our sins by becoming our substitute in death; and his resurrection, through which he demonstrates his triumph over death.
- We ought to rejoice in the accounts of the four gospels. In doing so we delight in the person, the power and the presence of the Lord Jesus.
- We must praise God for the book of Acts as we see how lives and theology were shaped by the life, death, burial and resurrection of Jesus.
- We should *dig deep* in the letters because they shed light upon all that God accomplished in Christ.
- We ought to stand in amazement as John takes us on a mind-blowing adventure in Revelation and gives us new and thrilling glimpses of the glorious Son of God.

In light of this I was reminded of an illustration used by Kevin DeYoung and Greg Gilbert in their excellent book, *What is the Mission of the Church?* The authors describe two kinds of people.

The first are *wide angle lens* people. These people are likely to give you a lengthy explanation concerning the nature of the gospel. They speak about the restoration of Eden, about social justice and acts of kindness. They speak about a New Heaven and a New Earth. The second group of people are *zoom lens* people. These people may provide a much briefer, even a *forensic* definition concerning the nature of the gospel. In short they will tell you what you need to believe in order to 'be saved'.[49]

Now, on occasions the Bible uses the word 'gospel' in both of these ways. Firstly, some texts provide us with a broader understanding of what God has planned through Jesus. In some ways the Nazareth Manifesto is one of these. Secondly, some texts, such as 1 Corinthians 15:1–8, describe an event through which we can be reconciled to God. I have come to realise that *wide angle lens* people, while attempting to understand the breadth of God's revelation, can on occasions miss that which is primary. However, *zoom lens* people can sometimes be so focused on the primary, that they miss its very context.

I want you to consider one more illustration. My latest mid-life crisis involves lycra and a carbon-fibre bike. One Friday afternoon, I noticed that my back wheel was badly buckled. This meant that unless it was fixed, I couldn't ride with my friends the following day. I posted a quick message on our WhatsApp group and immediately received a reply. Later that evening I took my wheel round to a friend's. He put it on a jig and set about showing me how to straighten it. The process was fairly simple. In the middle there was a hub and on the outside there was a rim. Then, there were a set of spokes that attached the rim to the hub. Simple! Over time some of these spokes had worked their way loose. So, under supervision I set about tightening them, one by one and little by little until the wheel ran true. Through the process I learned a very basic lesson. Essential to a smooth ride is a good relationship between the inner and the outer wheel. Coming back to the gospel, Tom Wright insightfully says, 'Everything pivots around the complex event that had happened: the Messiah died, was buried, was raised, was seen. Take that away and Christianity collapses. Put it in its proper place and the whole world is different. That is the news.'[50] I believe that's an essential statement. There is only good news if Jesus really died, in our place and for our sin. There is only hope if he was really buried and was really raised. Therefore, we all need to remember, if this truth is not central to all we say and all we do, then we are in for a very bumpy ride!

I am therefore convinced we need to, as far as we are able, define the gospel in such a way that we are in harmony with those who first announced it. Pete, who set the challenge to the ministry trainees, describes the gospel as, 'all that God has done in Jesus in order to reconcile sinful people to himself'. That's a great statement and ensures that we understand the life, substitutionary death, burial and resurrection of Jesus as the very heart of our faith.[51] It is the hub around which everything else is centred. But what about all the other good news that comes with the kingdom? John Piper puts it like this: 'that the blessings of the gospel should only be called gospel in relation to the cross.'[52] That's really important. We cannot emphasise the benefits of the gospel and dilute Jesus' death at Calvary. In his book *Center Church*, Timothy Keller reminds us, 'the results of the gospel should never be separated or confused with the gospel itself... Do not confuse what the gospel is with what the gospel does.'[53] Going back to our earlier illustration that helped us to view *euangelasathai* in a historical perspective. The *good news that brought great joy* was simple. The victory had been won. However, I am sure that the consequences of that victory were far-reaching and all-embracing. It meant that households were reunited, children played without fear, crops could be sown and that parties could be thrown.

As we reflect on the Nazareth Manifesto, we must trust that the gospel continues to come with supernatural power and causes social transformation. But let's be clear, social justice, racial harmony, caring for the poor, the care of orphans and widows and the welcoming of asylum seekers are all important expressions of the gospel. However, we must be careful not confuse them with the life-transforming message of the gospel.

DYNAMITE!

I love the fact that the word which Paul uses to describe the impact of the gospel is the very word from which we derive dynamite. Paul says to his friends in Rome that the gospel is according to 'the power (dynamis) of God that brings salvation to everyone who believes' (Romans 1:16).

As we consider the Nazareth Manifesto we remember that it was the Spirit who anointed Jesus to unleash this power. Then, sometime later Jesus promised his disciples, 'you will receive power when the Holy Spirit comes on you; and you will be my witnesses in Jerusalem, and in all Judea and Samaria, and to the ends of the earth' (Acts 1:8). Did you notice that? Neither Jesus nor the disciples proclaimed the gospel solely in their own strength. Rather, they did so with the anointing of the Spirit. I want to remind you, as we seek to serve God, there is *No Plan B*! God's plan and purpose is that you and I *do what we do and say what we say*, in the power of the Spirit. In doing so I believe we will then discover that even our service of him, is dependent upon him.

In the next chapter we will look at how this works in practice and look at practical ways in which we can follow.

CHAPTER FIVE

THE POOR

'Because he has anointed me to proclaim good news *to the poor.*' (Luke 4:18)

I trust we are in agreement. The gospel isn't just good news, its fabulous news. It doesn't bring a little joy, but great, incomparable and eternal joy. But let's not forget, taking the scroll of Isaiah, Jesus read, 'The Spirit of the Lord is on me, because he has anointed me to proclaim good news to the poor' (Luke 4:18). The news Jesus brought was specific news for specific people. The poor. In preparation for this chapter, I have just typed 'poor' into my online concordance. It revealed 176 references. By way of comparison I then typed in, 'cross'. Again, 176 references. The Bible says as much about the poor as it does the cross. Although, I remain convinced we are right to focus upon the cross, I also know how easy it is to ignore the poor. Therefore, before we begin, I feel prompted to share two confessions.

The first is this: I am loaded. Having completed a couple of surveys, I have discovered I am in the wealthiest 2% in the world.

When I get up, I have the option of heating, deciding what to wear and am spoiled by my choice of breakfast. I live in a nice house, drive a decent car, enjoy certain luxuries and have an annual holiday. The problem is, I don't always feel loaded. Because, all too often I compare myself with those who have more, instead of the majority with substantially less. Of course, I like to blame the media or advertisers for my perception. However, the Bible identifies the heart of my problem. Greed!

The second confession is worse, indeed, much worse. I feel ashamed to admit it, but I'm not sure if I really care about the poor. Having been involved in overseas ministry, I have seen some appalling sights. I have met children living in the sewers of Brazil and have sat by the lifeless body of an emaciated child in Romania. I have drunk *chai* with outreach workers in an Indian brothel and have observed the daily struggle of subsistence farmers in Tanzania. Lastly, I have visited South African townships, where children were gunned down as part of a gang initiation. However, in many ways my life continues as it did before. In fact to my shame, I have eaten dinner while watching a report about famine on the six o'clock news. So in light of the evidence, I don't know how much I care. I certainly know I don't care like God cares!

THE POOR IN THE OLD TESTAMENT

Looking at the breadth of Old Testament passages, we find the poor are naturally overlooked and exploited. I suspect we live in a similar society today. We respect those with wealth, power and influence. We admire those who portray the right image and have the right *stuff*. We disrespect those who don't. However, this overview of the Old Testament reveals two more insights.

The first is that the poor are protected by God. Time and again, God gives laws in order to curb the excesses of the wealthy and make provision for the poor.[54] Although wanting to avoid party politics, I share the following observation. Having read and re-read the Law of Moses, it appears God's plan was not to create a socialist utopia in Israel. However, I am equally convinced that God never intended to encourage unregulated capitalism among his people. Instead, God sought a nation in which the talented were rewarded and the vulnerable, protected; a society in which all would prosper. God's heart for the poor is again revealed through the Prophets. Whenever God's laws were disobeyed, he raised up those who would speak against injustice. During one time of particularly misplaced priorities, God spoke through Amos saying:

'I hate, I despise your religious festivals; your assemblies are a stench to me. Even though you bring me burnt offerings and grain offerings, I will not accept them. Though you bring choice fellowship offerings, I will have no regard for them. Away with the noise of your songs! I will not listen to the music of your harps. But let justice roll on like a river, righteousness like a never-failing stream!' (Amos 5:21–24)

Those are strong words which reveal God's priorities. I'm sure the people thought they were doing a fine job at observing their religion. Numbers were up, the singing was stirring and the preaching captivating. The problem was, however, God was far from pleased. Sadly, I suspect we can find ourselves in similar situations today. We become captivated by the latest song and get caught up with our latest spiritual experience. Yet, so easily we can forget God's heart for the poor.

Secondly, the poor received a promise. After Hannah dedicated her son Samuel at the temple, she prayed, saying, God 'raises the poor from the dust and lifts the needy from the ash heap' (1 Samuel 2:8). A few years later, David sang, 'The poor will eat and be satisfied' (Psalm 22:26). However through Isaiah we start to see how these promises to the poor will ultimately be fulfilled. Isaiah writes:

> 'The Spirit of the LORD will rest on him – the Spirit of wisdom and of understanding, the Spirit of counsel and of might, the Spirit of the knowledge and fear of the LORD – and he will delight in the fear of the LORD. He will not judge by what he sees with his eyes, or decide by what he hears with his ears; but with righteousness he will judge the needy, with justice he will give decisions for the poor of the earth'. (Isaiah 11:2–4)

As we know, this passage speaks of Jesus, his relationship with the Spirit and his heart for the poor. This heart is revealed again in Isaiah 61:1. This of course is the very passage that Jesus read in the synagogue in Nazareth. Jesus said he would 'bring good news to the poor'.

Finally, as we look closer at these two passages in Isaiah we discover something essential to our understanding of the poor. The word for poor that Isaiah uses is *anav*. This noun refers to the impoverished and afflicted, the humble and the meek. That's important. However, Isaiah isn't the only writer who uses this word. It is also used about Moses. God said: 'Now Moses was a very humble man, more humble (anav) than anyone else on the face of the earth' (Numbers 12:3). It's obvious by the context, God wasn't saying that Moses was the poorest man on the planet in terms of his material possessions. Rather, God was saying that despite his power and prestige, Moses wasn't full of his own self-importance. Moses was humble and meek.

So then, in the Old Testament we discover two kinds of poverty: economic poverty and spiritual poverty (or humility). However, all *the poor*, whether materially or spiritually poor, are assured of God's provision. They are promised a saviour and a wealth of blessings that he would bring.

JESUS' EXAMPLE

As a pastor it's my responsibility to teach about giving. I make a principle of doing this, not because the church needs money, but because giving is an expression of our obedience to Jesus. Over the years I have often based my teaching on Paul's second letter to the Corinthians. Here, the Corinthians are encouraged to give to the persecuted believers in Jerusalem. Paul gives them two examples from which they can learn. The first is the church in Macedonia, who, 'In the midst of a very severe trial, their overflowing joy and their extreme poverty welled up in rich generosity' (2 Corinthians 8:2). The second example is Jesus himself. Paul says, 'You know the generous grace of our Lord Jesus Christ. Though he was rich, yet for your sakes he became poor, so that by his poverty he could make you rich' (2 Corinthians 8:9). That is stunning. Paul reminds us of Jesus' journey from heaven to Earth. A descent that saw him exchange a throne for a manger. The adoration of angels for the rejection of the masses. A crown of glory for a crown of thorns. Paul also reminds us of the riches we receive because of Jesus' *poverty*. Riches that money could never purchase, riches such as forgiveness, adoption, relationship and eternity.

Although all four gospels reveal Jesus' message and seeming priority for the poor, it is probably Luke who draws most attention to it. So, given that we are looking at Luke 4:14–21, it is in Luke that we will stay. Right at the beginning of Luke's gospel we get a glimpse of what's to come. Whereas Matthew draws attention to the mysterious magi, Luke speaks about the stinking shepherds. Then, eight days after his birth, Jesus is taken to the temple to be circumcised. Here, mum and dad present an offering for Mary's purification, 'A pair of doves or two young pigeons' (Luke 2:24). This little detail reveals not only did Mary and Joseph observe the Law, but that they couldn't afford a lamb to sacrifice. They therefore took advantage of the provision for the poor made in Leviticus and offered what they could afford.[55] Isn't that wonderful? The one we now know as the King of Kings was born among the lowest of the low!

Although not mentioning poverty, I love the fact that Luke begins Jesus' genealogy by saying, 'He was the son, so it was thought, of Joseph' (Luke 3:23). Almost as an aside, we are reminded of the scandal around Jesus' birth and of his willingness to identify with those who were looked down on by others. This remains the pattern of Jesus' life. On one occasion Jesus reminds the crowd that they accused him of being 'a glutton and a drunkard, a friend of tax collectors and sinners' (Luke 7:34). I think this is worth dwelling on. A few years ago I bumped into a friend of mine. As usual my friend was drunk, his body wasted through neglect and the satanic tattoos visible across his face. While other people avoided him, I knew I should spend some time with him. So we sat on the curb, him with his vodka and me with my coffee. After a few minutes, our then-teenage daughter walked by with a group of friends. As soon as Sian saw me, she called over. Later that day I asked her how she felt when she saw her dad sat on a curb with a drunk in the middle of the day? She replied 'not much really, I guess it's just what you do.' Just so you know, I didn't feel affirmed by her, only convicted. You see that's not what my regular afternoon tends to look like. However, the truth is, I suspect it might have been a regular afternoon for Jesus. That is of course why he was called a *friend of sinners!* The benefit of these friendships can be seen through the story of Zacchaeus. There is something significant about Jesus' dealings with this vertically challenged tax-collector. Jesus invited himself for dinner, before not after Zacchaeus promised to recompense those he had swindled. I can only believe that it was Jesus' grace that led him to repentance.[56]

Having looked at Jesus' birth and life, we arrive at his death. At the turning point of history we see the means of creation[57], stripped naked and nailed to a block of wood. Of course Jesus wasn't the only person to be executed on Skull Hill that day.[58] There was someone to his left and someone to his right. On the cross Jesus chose to be identified with these two common criminals. One author movingly writes, 'His self-emptying was not a single loss or bereavement, but a growing poorer and poorer until at last nothing was left of Him but a piece of ground where he could weep and a cross whereon He could die. He renounced all that heart and flesh hold dear, until without friend or brother, without one tone of love, amid the mocking laughter of His slanderers, he gave up the ghost'.[59]

JESUS' INSTRUCTIONS

Again we are spoiled for choice as to which passages we examine. Indeed, Jesus speaks more about money than about prayer. However, before we start, I want to share a brief story. A few weeks ago I had the privilege of baptising a young man who had just come to Christ. As I so often do with new believers, I encouraged him to read the gospel of Luke, one chapter a day for twenty-four days. At the end of his reading he asked me a brilliant question, 'Does God struggle with me for being wealthy?' The question clearly revealed that he had taken the words of Jesus seriously. Therefore, following my friend's example, let's not skip over uncomfortable passages. Instead, let's stop and face the challenge that Jesus' words still bring.

The most famous message ever preached was delivered on an unknown hillside in Galilee. Through the Sermon on the Mount Jesus tells us who will be blessed in the kingdom of God: the poor, the hungry, the sorrowful, the hated and the rejected.[60] In translating Jesus' words from Aramaic into Greek, both Matthew and Luke choose the same word for poor. This word *ptochoi*, literally means 'to crouch or cower like a beggar'. Interestingly, in his account, Matthew refers to the *poor in Spirit*.[61] In societies that look up to those with power and prestige, how could those whose spirits resemble the posture of a beggar be blessed? Don Carson helpfully reminds us, 'We must come to him (God) and acknowledge our spiritual bankruptcy, emptying ourselves of our self-righteousness, moral esteem and personal vanity. Emptied of these things we are ready for him to fill us.'[62] It is only when we acknowledge our need of him that we receive God's grace.[63]

Having just visited my local supermarket I decided to take a quick look at the magazines. A frightening number seemed dedicated to the lives and loves of the rich and famous. The covers adorned with smiling royalty, bikini-clad celebrities and stars on red carpets. Jesus tells a parable about a rich farmer who had a bumper crop and decided to 'Take life easy; eat, drink and be merry' (Luke 12:19). I guess he was the kind of guy to make these front covers. However, Jesus tells us, 'God said to him, "You fool! This very night your life will be demanded from you. Then who will get what you have prepared for yourself?" This is how it will be with whoever stores up things for themselves but is not rich towards God' (Luke 12:20–21). I hope you have noticed, the kingdom of God comes with a unique set of values. It is a kingdom in which beggars are invited to banquets.[64] Where a broke widow contributing a few coppers is said to have given more than publicity-seeking millionaires.[65] It is a kingdom in which Jesus names a poor man whose sores were licked by dogs, but not the wealthy man at whose gates he begged.[66]

Lastly, Luke tells us about a rich young ruler who came to Jesus. The man appeared sincere in asking how he could inherit eternal life. It seemed this man had kept the Law since being a little lad. But Jesus challenged him saying, 'sell everything you have and give it to the poor, and you will have treasure in heaven' (Luke 18:22). I still find what Jesus said shocking. However, the thing that impacts me most is the fact that Jesus allowed the man to walk away. He didn't pursue him, nor did he *water down* the instruction. Given the exchange it's little wonder Jesus said it was 'easier for a camel to go through the eye of a needle than a rich man to enter the kingdom of God' (Luke 18:25). I suspect Jesus spoke with a wry grin. But the truth remains. It's easier to drive a double-decker bus through a hula-hoop than a wealthy person to get into glory.

Coming back to our starting point: if the gospel is good news for the poor, is it bad news for the wealthy? It certainly is if we the wealthy treasure our possessions more than we do Jesus. It is if we are not willing to identify with the poor and learn from the poor. It is if we are too tight-fisted to give to the poor. Given these reflections, it is little wonder that Paul reminded his friend Timothy, it is the 'love of money' which 'is a root of all kinds of evil' (1 Timothy 6:10).

FIVE CHALLENGES TO THE CHURCH

Before we move on, I want to raise five practical challenges we all face as we consider how the gospel is good news for the poor. Although each one ought to be explored at length, time and space mean that we can only refer to them briefly.

1. We are called to follow Jesus' example and to obey his teaching

This challenge was obviously taken up by the early church. Luke describes how the believers met daily. How they broke bread and prayed together. He tells us they had 'everything in common' and 'sold their possessions' and gave 'to those in need' (Acts 3:42–47). But notice when this happened. It was after the outpouring of the Spirit at Pentecost. Giving to the poor was not distinct from the work of the Spirit. It was an evidence of the work of the Spirit. When James, Peter and John commission Paul and Barnabas to preach to the Gentiles, their only request was 'that they remember the poor' (Galatians 2:10). Again, giving to the poor wasn't a distraction from the gospel. It was an outworking of the gospel.

2. We are called to proclamation and demonstration

Over the years the church's priorities have swung like a pendulum. For a time we have focused solely on proclamation. Then all change, the Word is out and social action is in! But, Jesus doesn't ask us to choose one and ditch the other. You may know that the only one of Jesus' miracles recorded in all four gospels is the Feeding of the Five Thousand. So let's be reminded of its purpose. At its most basic level, Jesus fed hungry people. On another level, this action enabled Jesus to teach those who were not distracted by the rumble of their stomachs. Then lastly, the miracle served as a sign of something greater. Jesus didn't just speak of love; he demonstrated love. The miracle acted as a remarkable *sign*, that the one who multiplied a little lad's lunch, was himself the 'bread of life' (John 6:35). The ministry of Jesus is not then, word *or* deed. The ministry of Jesus is word *and* deed.[67] So let's be clear, if we tell people about God's love, but don't demonstrate it, then they may not believe us. On the other hand, if we give our lives to social action, but never mention the gospel, we may leave people well-fed, but still without a Saviour!

3. We are called to be good stewards

I was raised during the Cold War when people referred to the First and Third World. There were two extremes, prosperity and poverty. Although statistics indicate absolute poverty has reduced significantly, it is still unacceptably high. However, over recent years we have been introduced to a new category of poverty: relative poverty. It is an acknowledgment that there are those in our neighbourhood who, although not absolutely poor, are relatively poor. They can buy food, but not healthy food. They have a roof, but their walls are damp. Their children are at school, but have no access to wi-fi for homework.[68] So given our finite resources and the apparent infinite need, to whom do we give?[69]

We all need to struggle with the question, be convinced by Scripture and led by the Spirit. Having done so over the years, I have rightly or wrongly concluded the following:

- To give, where possible, to churches and Christian charities which are committed to both proclamation and demonstration
- To build relationships with those we support on the basis that I have a responsibility to learn as well as to give
- That I have a responsibility to those in relative poverty as well as those in absolute poverty

4. We are granted different abilities with which to serve

I believe it is helpful to understand different areas of social concern. Ronald Sider helpfully distinguishes three. Firstly, relief, which is required whenever there is a crisis, whether caused through natural or human means. Secondly, development, which is the coming alongside of others in order to facilitate their own growth and sustainability. Lastly, structural change, which seeks to address the building blocks of society through politics and economics.[70] My point is this. As believers we are called to represent Jesus and serve the poor. For some that will be serving in the local Food Bank and for others it will be speaking on matters of social justice at the United Nations. What matters most, however, is that we use the talents that God has entrusted to us for the good of others and for the glory of God.[71]

5. We are called to create a church for all

A few years back, a local man who had given his life to Christ rolled up to a church I was involved with. Being a caring community he was immediately invited out to lunch the next week. The following Sunday he was driven in a big car to a big house where he was sat at a big table. Having eaten a large roast meal and consumed a glass of fine wine, he was then dropped back home. Despite the wonderful hospitality, he never returned to the church. He later told someone there was no problem with the people at the church, but they were just not like him. We must to ensure that we are mindful of people's backgrounds, cultures and preferences in order to ensure our churches are accessible for all. Although Paul was thankful that the *wall of hostility* was torn down between Jew and Gentile,[72] so often the barriers between rich and poor remain within our church communities.

NO PLAN B

THE NEED OF THE SPIRIT

If you were to ask your non-believing friends and family what they want out of life, I guess their answers would fall into three main categories. People want to be healthy, wealthy and happy. In many ways, so do I. However, we must be careful not to rewrite the Scriptures and try to make them guarantee all three. Instead, we must recognise that Jesus calls us to a life of obedience and of sacrifice. In light of this I need the Spirit. I need him to convict me of my greed, apathy, complacency and my own self-seeking. I need the Spirit in order to conform me to the likeness of Jesus.

In closing I want to share a moving story that has remained with me for many years. In 1873 a young Catholic priest left his home in Belgium in order to serve the people of Molokai. Today this Pacific island is a tourist trap, but in Damien's time it served as a leper colony. Father Damien empowered the people to build schools, houses and hospitals. With his own hands he built coffins and dug graves. After eleven years of ministry, Damien accidentally poured boiling water onto his foot. Although the foot blistered, he felt no pain. The next Sunday morning, Damien climbed the steps of the pulpit. Damien had preached to lepers on numerous occasions, but this was the first time he had spoken as a leper. On the April 15, 1889, Father Damien died of his disease. Although his body was repatriated to Belgium his right arm was buried on Molokai. It was remembered as 'the hand that went forth to help'. That is a staggering testimony, of a man who gave himself for the poor. Yet any testimony we offer or example we cite is only a poor shadow in comparison to the one we see in Jesus.

THE POOR

In light of this I leave you with the words of this lovely hymn:

Thou who wast rich beyond all splendour,
All for love's sake becamest poor;
Thrones for a manger didst surrender,
Sapphire-paved courts for stable floor.
Make us what thou wouldst have us be.
Thou who art love beyond all telling,
Saviour and King, we worship thee.[73]

CHAPTER SIX

PRISONERS

'He has sent me to proclaim freedom for the prisoners'
(Luke 4:18)

Have you ever wondered how many prisoners Jesus actually set free? There are no accounts of him storming the Fortress Antonio in Jerusalem or leading a breakout from the cells in Galilea. Yet, at the synagogue in Nazareth, Jesus said he was anointed 'to proclaim freedom for the prisoners' (Luke 4:18). In order to answer this question, let me share a brief illustration. As a child I climbed some of the more accessible mountains of Snowdonia. Time and again, my brother David and I would run ahead of our parents in order to be the first to the top. However, I remember how we would arrive at our destination, only to realise we still had a distance to go. Any experienced walker knows the frustration of false summits with the true peak being concealed for much of the journey. In some ways this is how certain Old Testament prophecies reveal God's truth. They unfold one vista after another, each more glorious than the last. With that in mind, let's stand back and look at the *three peaks* of Isaiah 61.

As we know, the words Jesus read at the synagogue in Nazareth were initially penned by Isaiah in 700 BC. The prophet introduces himself as 'The LORD's anointed' (Isaiah 61:1). He said, as a consequence of their rebellion, God's people would be taken into exile in Babylon. However, God wouldn't abandon them, but would guarantee their safe return. Then, through many of the prophets, including Jeremiah, Ezekiel, Daniel, Ezra and Nehemiah, we discover that what God promised, God delivered. Physical prisoners were granted physical freedom. The people returned.

However, once back in their homeland it became apparent that this prophecy revealed another truth which had been previously hidden. Isaiah's words also spoke about the coming Messiah. This prophecy, in part realised through the return from exile, would find another and a greater fulfilment in Jesus. However, the freedom that Jesus brought was very different than the return from Babylon. The freedom Jesus brought was primarily, but not exclusively, spiritual.

Once Jesus began to teach, something else came into view that could not possibly be seen before. Jesus revealed that this would not be his only visit. Therefore, we now know some of the words of Isaiah 61 were not to be fulfilled during Jesus' earthly ministry, but will instead be fulfilled upon his return.

Now let's come back to where we started. *How many prisoners did Jesus actually set free?* I believe the answer to the question is multitudes. We will look specifically at the subject of healing and deliverance in subsequent chapters. However, I want to now look at one well-known story which is found in Luke 8:40–55.[74]

PRISONERS

In this passage we will see how Jesus released a woman from her particular prison and in doing so, restored her rightful inheritance.

SCENE ONE: A DESPERATE REQUEST

Let's start by setting the scene. It had been eighteen months since the launch of his manifesto in Nazareth and Jesus had been busy, very busy! Jesus, supported by his disciples, had found much favour, if not a little opposition from the people. Wherever he went, the crowds came to hear, to see, or to witness a miracle. Having delivered a demonised man east of Galilee, Jesus returned to Capernaum, a little fishing village, just thirty miles northeast of Nazareth. As the boat approached the shore, Jesus would have seen the crowd that had gathered, expectantly. It is here that we first meet Jairus, a leader of the local synagogue.

Given the importance of the synagogue in Jewish life, Jairus would have been a man of high standing. However, Luke tells us that he 'fell at Jesus' feet' and 'pleaded with him' to come to his house. The reason for his distress was obvious. His twelve-year-old daughter was dying. Mark tells us Jairus called her his 'little daughter' (Mark 5:23). I remember how, when our daughter hit four, she insisted on being called a *big girl*. I guess that if Jairus' daughter was healthy and in earshot, he may have chosen another phrase. However, she wasn't and he was desperate. She may have been twelve, but her dad still viewed her as his *little girl*. As Jesus made his way to the home of Jairus, the crowds nearly crushed him. I can picture the fear on the faces of the disciples as much as the excitement of the crowd. However, I can't imagine the turmoil in which Jairus found himself. Although Jesus had agreed to go with him, time must have seemed against them. Then, without warning or prior announcement, Jesus stopped.

SCENE TWO: AN UNEXPECTED INTERRUPTION

Whenever I read this extraordinary passage, I am reminded of how one commentator breaks the unexpected interruption into three distinct parts: faith concealed, faith rewarded and faith revealed.[75] As we continue the story I want us to consider these three things.

1. Faith concealed

As soon as Jesus stopped he asked the question: 'who touched me?' Imagine a celebrity on the red carpet asking the world's paparazzi, 'who took my photo?'[76] The answer would be, 'we all did'. Although Peter was polite in his response, I suspect he thought Jesus had asked a stupid question. They had all touched him. But Jesus knew someone had touched him, specifically, intentionally and in faith!

Luke continues, 'And a woman was there who had been subject to bleeding for twelve years, but no one could heal her. She came up behind him and touched the edge of his cloak' (Luke 8:43–44). Think for a moment about where you were or what you were doing twelve years ago. I suspect that a lot has changed in that time. However, for this woman there is a sense in which nothing had changed. There had been no regular menstrual cycle, just a constant discharge, month after month and year after year. For any woman, in any society, this would have been debilitating. But for this woman, in this society, it must have felt like a prison sentence.

Let me explain. According to the Law of Moses, a woman was considered as *unclean* for seven days of her regular period. Anything she lay on, sat on, or touched would be seen as *unclean*. If her discharge continued above seven days she would remain *unclean* for as long as it lasted. For twelve years this woman would have been excluded from community life, been barred from the local synagogue and banned from the temple in Jerusalem. If she lived in a devout household she would have had her own seat, her own bed and her own eating utensils. She would have no doubt lived under shame and guilt. Again, Mark gives us a surprising insight. He says, 'she had suffered a great deal under the care of many doctors and had spent all she had, yet instead of getting better she grew worse' (Mark 5:24). Having read a few first-century cures for excessive bleeding, I have decided not to include them here. Although some are amusing, others are toe-curling and none of them worked! The fact this woman was willing to spend her money on such hopeless treatments gives us a glimpse into her desperation. The fact that she ventured out, battled through the crowd and reached out to Jesus, gives us a glimpse of her faith and desperation. It is probable that she simply touched one of the four tassels that would have been attached to Jesus' shawl. These were intended to remind Jewish men of their responsibility to obey the Law of Moses.[77] As these tassels were often more prominent on the shawls of rabbis they were sometimes seen to have mystical powers. It's not surprising then, that on a number of occasions the crowds would simply reach out to touch the hem of Jesus' garments in order to receive their healing.[78]

Jesus stopped for one reason, he knew that *power* had gone out of him. So what was this *power* that Jesus referred to? The answer becomes obvious when we look at what has been said before.

Luke tells us that Jesus had 'returned to Galilee in the power of the Spirit' (Luke 4:14) and that 'the power of the Lord was with Jesus to heal those who were ill' (Luke 5:17). Then, 'the people all tried to touch him, because power was coming from him and healing them all' (Luke 6:19). According to Luke, *power* and the Spirit appear to be synonymous. Therefore the power that had left Jesus in order to bring healing to this woman was the *power* of the Spirit. There may well be times when we, or those we pray for, experience physical manifestations. These manifestations may range from the experience of warmth, a tingling sensation, shaking or even falling over. In the same way, someone may cry when they are sad or laugh when they are happy, these manifestations are indicators of a deeper reality. Although I don't believe we should pursue these manifestations in and of themselves, we should rejoice whenever we experience or witness evidence of the Spirit's work.

I suspect that the woman had tried to sneak up behind Jesus in order to receive her healing. I also guess she then wanted to simply slip away into the shadows. However, Jesus had other ideas.

2. Faith rewarded

As soon as the woman touched Jesus, 'her bleeding stopped.' I love that. She didn't go away wondering if she would feel better in the morning, nor did she improve over a period of time. Instead, she was immediately released from the infirmity that had bound her for twelve long years. Now, according to *the letter of the Law*, Jesus would have been made ceremonially *unclean* by this woman. However, we have just read that due to her meeting Jesus, she had been miraculously made clean. The same is true of the man suffering from leprosy who Jesus touched just a few chapters earlier.[79] Again, instead of Jesus becoming *unclean* through his contact with a leper, the man became unblemished. Every so often I meet Christians who seem intent on living under the Old Covenant. They seem forever caught up with rules and regulations, with guilt and condemnation. I think that this passage gloriously illustrates how Jesus has superseded all that which has gone before. This truth wants me to live in the fullness of the New Covenant, not in the shadow of the Old.

So when the woman realised that she couldn't stay hidden any longer, she stepped forward. In fear and in trembling she made her way to Jesus. Every eye in the crowd would have been fixed upon her, as she then knelt at Jesus' feet. In many ways I believe what happened next was better than what had gone before. Jesus said, 'Daughter, your faith has healed you. Go in peace' (Luke 8:48). I have no idea how old this woman was. Whether she was older or younger than Jesus is unimportant. What matters is how Jesus' heart is revealed for her. In the same way Jairus was concerned for his *little girl*, so Jesus was filled with compassion for his *daughter.* Jesus blessed her for her faith and granted her peace. In our society we tend to think of peace as the absence of trouble, or war, or hostility. In Jewish society, peace is not the absence of something, it is the presence of something. The Hebrew word for peace, 'shalom', is still used as a greeting to this day. Jesus didn't just take away the infirmity, he replaced it with completeness, spiritual prosperity and wholeness. He granted her *shalom.* I believe that this is God's plan for each of us. Jesus doesn't just take away our guilt, he gives us his righteousness. He doesn't simply remove our fear, but replaces it with assurance. He doesn't only release us from prison, but grants us his freedom. God wants us to know his deep and assuring *shalom.*

3. Faith revealed

I believe there are three reasons why Jesus wanted this woman's faith to be revealed. The first is that faith is important to God. Some years later, the writer to the Hebrews would say, 'without faith it is impossible to please God, because anyone who comes to him must believe that he exists and that he rewards those who earnestly seek him' (Hebrews 11:6). We cannot please God by depending on our own understanding, experience or abilities. The only way we can please him is by depending on him. Jesus stopped and asked, 'who touched me?' I don't believe that Jesus said this to satisfy his curiosity. I believe that he said it on order to affirm the woman who had *reached out in faith.*

Secondly, it was important for this woman that her faith was revealed. She had spent twelve years infirmed and possibly ashamed. Now, here in full public view she was honoured. For what? Simply for reaching out to Jesus.

Lastly, it's important that her faith was revealed for us. When we read the rest of Hebrews Chapter 11 we find many more examples of God honouring those who reached out in faith. Just like this woman, their lives are given as examples from which we can learn and be inspired. I suspect that if we are honest, we would all admit that there are times when our faith isn't as strong as we would like it to be. However, incredibly Jesus says we don't need a lot of faith, just a little. Jesus said that faith the size of a mustard seed is able to move a mountain.[80] In the 21st century we might say, it's not the size of the button that determines the magnitude of the explosion, it's the power of the warhead! Whenever we reach out in faith, however fearfully or tentatively, we do so believing that God is able to move in power. Whenever we reach out in faith, I believe God wants to bless us, just as he did this woman. Over the years there has been much discussion concerning the relationship between our faith and the will of God. Although space does not permit us to explore this here, I do want to share a brief story.

Only recently I attended the funeral of a friend and colleague. This godly and humble man died in what seemed to be the prime of life. From the moment he fell ill, those who loved him prayed for his full recovery. However, as we gathered to say goodbye, his family and friends remained full of faith. Despite their grief, they still raised their hands to heaven and praised God for his faithfulness. Faith is about trusting God in each and every circumstance. It's an acknowledgement that although there are times we don't understand God's will and purpose, Jesus continues to rule and to reign.[81]

SCENE THREE: MISSION ACCOMPLISHED

Let's give a brief thought for Jairus. His hopes must have soared when Jesus agreed to accompany him home. Then, just as they neared his daughter's bedside, there was this interruption. I have no idea how long it was, but for Jairus it must have felt like a lifetime. Just when he thought it couldn't get any worse, it did. 'While Jesus was still speaking, someone came from the house of Jairus, the synagogue leader. "Your daughter is dead," he said. "Don't bother the teacher anymore"' (Luke 8:49). I guess for us, this would have been the end. But, for Jesus, it was simply the beginning. He assured Jairus of the outcome and followed him home. Then Jesus, along with Jairus, his wife, Peter, James and John entered the little girl's room. I love what Jesus did and said next. There was no shouting and no drama. However, with absolute assurance, Jesus took the girl's hand and said 'my child, get up'. As he did, 'her spirit returned' (Luke 8:54–55).

It often strikes me when I read the gospels that Jesus never appeared to be rushed or hurried by others. Take for example the time he heard his friend Lazarus was sick. Jesus 'stayed where he was for two more days' (John 11:6). Then there is this occasion. Despite being committed to the request of the synagogue leader, Jesus stopped to meet the needs of an unknown woman. So what was Jesus' secret and how can we learn from his example? For a start Jesus said, 'I tell you, the Son can do nothing by himself; he can do only what he sees his Father doing, because whatever the Father does, the Son does also' (John 5:19).[82] That's a remarkable statement. The Son of God who spoke galaxies into being is confessing his dependence upon his Father. Jesus didn't act as an independent operator. Instead, throughout his life we see evidenced God the Father, God the Son and God the Spirit working as one. For this reason, Jesus was always willing to be led by the Spirit. When Paul instructs us to 'live (or walk) by the Spirit' (Galatians 5:16), I don't believe he is trotting out a meaningless cliché. He is encouraging us to live like Jesus.

Just a quick reminder. We have looked at this story to see how Jesus proclaimed *freedom for prisoners*. The God who enabled his people to return from exile, enabled Jesus to release this woman from her captivity, a father to be freed from grief and a young girl to be delivered from death. In the same way, God wants to use us to bring freedom to others.

FREEDOM FROM...

The first and most obvious way in which Jesus brings freedom is to release us from our circumstances. Many years ago I was preaching in what was then our home church in Rochdale. At the end of my message, I made an offer to anyone who wanted to meet Jesus for the first time, to come forward. I remember one young man in his mid-twenties walking to the front. I had spoken to him a lot over the previous few weeks, but hadn't known the depth of his struggle. The man told me about the pain of his childhood, how he had started to drink and how he became addicted to heroin. I led him in a simple prayer and listened as he asked the Lord for forgiveness and acceptance. At the end of his prayer we simply stood in silence. It felt an age had gone by when I eventually asked, 'how do you feel?' I can almost hear his answer now. He simply said, 'I have never felt clean before.' Isn't that fabulous?

Sometimes, however, God wants us to do more than pray with people. He wants us to work practically on their behalf. I recently spoke at a pastors' conference in the Indian state of Karnataka. While talking to the pastors over lunch, I discovered many of them were involved in a ministry to *devadasis*. I apologised about my ignorance and asked our host who these people were. He explained how young girls are handed over to the priests of Hindu temples, where they are expected to serve as prostitutes. Although this practice has been illegal in India since 1988 it remains prevalent in some Southern provinces. My friend told me these girls are kept in poverty, abused daily and when they reach forty are 'worth less than shit'. The glorious thing was, these churches didn't only tell these women about the love of God, they demonstrated it. Despite the danger they put themselves in, they offered escape routes and employment. They made it possible for these women to leave the *prison* in which they lived. Over the years many devadasis have left the temples and entered meaningful employment and a fair percentage are now members of local church families. Jesus still sets people free!

FREEDOM IN...

It's fabulous when Jesus releases people from their circumstances. However, it's just as impressive when he brings freedom to people's hearts and lives. In Acts Chapter 16, we find Paul and Silas again in trouble, this time in the town of Philippi. They had upset the locals by casting out an evil spirit from a slave girl, who made her owners money through predicting the future. Paul and Silas were arrested, stripped, beaten and thrown in prison. Although I have never been in their situation, I suspect my response may be significantly different to theirs. Luke tells us 'About midnight Paul and Silas were praying and singing hymns to God' (Acts 16:25). Isn't that extraordinary? They weren't whingeing, complaining or discussing the miscarriage of justice. They weren't even praying for their release, they were praising God. Just then there was an earth-quake. The prison doors flung open and prisoners' chains became loose. The Roman jailor would have been responsible to guard the prisoners at the cost of his own life. Even if one had got away, he would have faced execution from the authorities. Seeing he was about to fall on his sword, Paul assured him that all the prisoners were still present. After witnessing their faith, the jailor said 'what must I do to be saved?' (Luke 16:30). The point I want to make is simple. Paul and Silas were battered but not broken. They were chained, but not captive. They found freedom even within the toughest of circumstances. I am privileged to have witnessed firsthand the amazing work of Message South Africa, led by my good friend Tim Tucker. I have also met a number of those who have come to faith while *inside* through their prison ministry. These men and women are living testimonies to the truth that real freedom can only come through the gospel of Jesus.

I want therefore to encourage those who have prayed to be freed from their circumstances, but continue to struggle in them. Recently I was at a meeting where we sang the wonderful song by Aaron Keyes, *Sovereign Over Us.* I believe God's sovereignty simply means that nothing happens in time or space that God does not purpose or permit and will use for his glory. That is a difficult, but wonderful truth. As we sang together, I remembered how God had used this song to encourage me through a really tough time some years ago. I also realised that it was this *big view* of God which encouraged Paul through his many trials.[83] Although there will always be things that we don't understand, we can still rejoice in the God who is greater than our circumstances. As the song says, 'Your plans are still to prosper, You have not forgotten us, You're with us in the fire and the flood. Faithful forever, Perfect in love. You are sovereign over us.'[84] Given then his willingness to worship, even with fresh wounds weeping, it is little wonder Paul tells his friends in Corinth, 'Now the Lord is the Spirit, and where the Spirit of the Lord is, there is freedom' (2 Corinthians 3:17).

NO PLAN B

Something struck me not long ago. There was one literal, physical prisoner that Jesus set free. His name of course was Barabbas. After Jesus' arrest, Pilate, the local Roman ruler admitted he could find no reason to charge him. Therefore, Pilate empowered the people to decide who lived and who died. The choice was stark. They must decide between Jesus, or a murderer by the name of Barabbas. However, the whole crowd shouted, 'Away with this man! Release Barabbas to us!' (Luke 23:18). In the same way Jesus took the place of Barabbas on the cross at Calvary, so he took your place and mine. Paul says 'God made him who had no sin to be sin for us, so that in him we might become the righteousness of God' (2 Corinthians 5:21). That's the *good news that brings great joy.*

As I talk to people in my community who don't yet know Jesus, I am aware of the things which hold them captive. Some seem bound by fears, bitterness, arrogance or pride. Others are bound in unhappy marriages or in self-destructive cycles. In the same way the Spirit anointed Jesus to bring freedom to others, so I believe he wants to anoint us. God wants to give us a new confidence in the gospel and bolder faith in which to walk. God to use us in order that we, like Jesus, may see many prisoners set free!

CHAPTER SEVEN

BLIND SIGHT

'...and recovery of sight for the blind' (Luke 4:18)

I recently found a battered copy of John Wimber's *Power Evangelism* on my bookshelf. As I picked it up, some of the pages fell onto the floor. After gathering them up, I set about putting them back in order. While doing so, I read something I had last looked at twenty five years ago. Wimber wrote 'almost half of all the verses in the gospels involve some sort of power encounter, with healing accounting for from nine to twenty per cent.'[85] Healing was not an add-on to Jesus' ministry, but an intrinsic expression of it. However, as we come to the statement in Jesus' manifesto concerning the 'recovery of sight for the blind' (Luke 4:18), we must ask the question, 'Who were the blind to whom Jesus referred?' In previous chapters we saw that the *poor* could be either economically disadvantaged or spiritually humble. We also found that *prisoners* could be either physically or spiritually bound. Although Jesus restored the sight of the physically blind, through looking at the following story, we will also discover how this enabled spiritual eyes to be opened! Luke writes:

> As Jesus approached Jericho, a blind man was sitting by the roadside begging. When he heard the crowd going by, he asked what was happening. They told him, 'Jesus of Nazareth is passing by.' He called out, 'Jesus, Son of David, have mercy on me!' Those who led the way rebuked him and told him to be quiet, but he shouted all the more, 'Son of David, have mercy on me!' Jesus stopped and ordered the man to be brought to him. When he came near, Jesus asked him, 'What do you want me to do for you?' 'Lord, I want to see,' he replied. Jesus said to him, 'Receive your sight; your faith has healed you.' Immediately he received his sight and followed Jesus, praising God. When all the people saw it, they also praised God. (Luke 18:35–43)

Although wanting to focus on Luke's gospel, it's worth reading the two parallel accounts, in Matthew 20:20–34 and Mark 10:46–52. In doing so we discover more detail including the man's name. Once, when I preached from this story, I asked the congregation if anyone knew what their name meant. Those who answered shared how their names all had positive meanings. Not this man, according to Mark: his name was Bartimaeus, *the son of the unclean one*. It was Jewish custom that names would be prophetic, often speaking a blessing over a person's life. But Bartimaeus' name only served as a curse.[86] As he woke on the morning in question, I suspect the *son of the unclean one* had no idea about what would happen. Instead he had just one hope, that he would receive enough loose change, to buy enough food, to *tide him over* until the following day. However, this seemingly ordinary day was destined to end in the most extraordinary way. This was the day Bartimaeus would meet Jesus. Their encounter took place as Jesus made his final journey to Jerusalem. As he travelled, accompanied by his disciples, Jesus stopped at the ancient city of Jericho. Although Bartimaeus may have never seen Jesus, he had obviously heard about him. As Jesus passed by, Bartimaeus called out, 'Jesus, Son of David, have mercy on me!' The crowds said 'button it'. But Bartimaeus persevered and Jesus answered. The rest they say is history!

1. Bartimaeus receives revelation

It is obvious that Bartimaeus didn't just believe Jesus was *worth a go*. When he called out to him, he used the title the *Son of David*. This was a title used of the one who would be descended from King David, who would establish his kingdom for eternity. It was a name given to the coming Messiah. Next we see Bartimaeus is convinced that Jesus could restore his sight. In doing so, he again acknowledges Jesus as Messiah. In the Old Testament people had been healed of various sicknesses, including leprosy. However, it was believed that only the Messiah would bring sight to the blind.[87]

As we read the story, I believe we are right to marvel at Bartimaeus' persistence. We should also remember though, Jesus had previously said that 'no one can come to me unless the Father who sent me draws them to me' (John 6:44). So here, we witness a man responding in faith in a most dramatic way as he is supernaturally drawn to Jesus. Once Bartimaeus was summoned by Jesus, Mark tells us, he 'threw his cloak aside' (Mark 10:50). That may not sound a big deal for us, but I guess Bartimaeus didn't have many possessions. He did however possess a cloak to keep him warm in winter and to act as shade in summer. Over the years, many have suggested the civil authorities would hand out cloaks to beggars in order to sanction their activities. In some ways they would act as authorisation in the way that those selling the Big Issue now wear a lanyard badge. Although I can't find any evidence of this, if true then Bartimaeus was at the point of no return. I am convinced each of us needs to ensure that nothing gets in the way and nothing acts as a hindrance in our pursuit of Jesus. We each need to come to the point of no return.

2. Bartimaeus receives grace

Here we are privileged to witness one of the most amazing meetings of all time. The *son of the unclean one* is brought before the Son of God. Then, the Son of God asks, 'What do you want from me?' (vs 41) That's a brilliant question. All day, every day, Bartimaeus would ask passers-by for change. But now he asked for something he had never asked for before. He replied 'Lord, I want to see'. I love the fact that Jesus' response is as straightforward as his question. Jesus said, 'Receive your sight; your faith has healed you' (vs 42). Don't you just love the grace of God? Paul writes to his friends in Ephesus, 'For it is by grace you have been saved, through faith – and this is not from yourselves, it is the gift of God' (Ephesians 2:8). Bartimaeus received sight. Why? Because God granted him the faith, by which he could respond. Don't you find that incredible? Don't you also find it most humbling, that we like Bartimaeus are totally and utterly dependent on God's unearned, unmerited and undeserved favour?

3. Bartimaeus continued to follow

The gospels don't tell us if Bartimaeus was born blind or whether he became blind later in life. However, a part of me wants to believe the former. Because if so, the first person Bartimaeus ever saw was Jesus. Now, we must remember that he saw more than a prophet and more than a healer. Bartimaeus saw the Saviour. It is little wonder then that Luke tells us that, having received his sight, Bartimaeus 'followed Jesus, praising God' (vs 42). The fact that Bartimaeus directed his praise to heaven reminds us of the fact that Jesus' healing ministry served a greater goal. Douglas Macmillan expresses this brilliantly by writing, 'While he (Jesus) clearly sympathised with ill people and loved them very deeply and set out to help them, he had come to deal with the greater, even uglier reality which underlay all suffering and illness – sin. He had come to redeem us from the penalty and power of sin'.[88] Jesus' physical healing of Bartimaeus, however wonderful it was, points us to a greater reality. That the one who opened his eyes physically was the one who brought illumination to his heart. There is another glorious example of this in John's gospel which uses Jesus' healing of a blind man in John 9 as a sign to point us to Jesus' claim to be 'the light of the world' (John 9:5).

We have seen how Jesus' healing ministry was both intrinsic to his mission and testified to his identity. However, given the purpose of this book, it is important that we explore the means by which Jesus healed, before discovering the implications for us.

NO PLAN B

THE SPIRIT WHO HEALED THROUGH JESUS

There are no records in Scripture of Jesus healing the sick until after the Spirit descended upon him at his baptism.[89] Jesus then returned to Nazareth in the 'power of the Spirit' (Luke 4:14) and declared the Spirit would anoint him to bring 'recovery of sight to the blind' (Luke 4:18). It is worth considering this further. This means that Jesus didn't heal a cough or a splutter, never mind a blind man, until he was around thirty years old. Why? Because, Jesus didn't do what he did, or say what he said, because of his deity. Rather, Jesus did what he did and said what he said through the power of the Spirit. In order to highlight this, Matthew records an occasion where Jesus 'healed all their sick'. He then says this was to 'fulfil what was spoken through the prophet Isaiah: 'Here is my servant whom I have chosen, the one I love, in whom I delight; I will put my Spirit on him' (Matthew 12:15,17–18). In order to better understand how Jesus healed in the power of the Spirit, I want to look briefly at two passages.

Firstly, 'One day Jesus was teaching, and Pharisees and teachers of the law were sitting there. They had come from every village of Galilee and from Judea and Jerusalem. And the power of the Lord was with Jesus to heal those who were ill' (Luke 5:17)

This verse is found just prior to the staggering story involving four friends and a paralysed man. The scene is almost comical. Unable to get their friend to Jesus because of the crowds, these four men made their way onto the roof of the house where Jesus was. If Jesus was teaching at the time, I suspect he could no longer be heard because of the banging above. Rubble began to fall. Then, daylight appeared as this desperate man was lowered on a makeshift bed by his mates. The men's desperation is obvious, as is the reason for it. This was an occasion when Jesus' healing ministry appeared to be in *full flow*. This may be a shock to some, but I don't believe this was always true. I am not suggesting that healing was not a massive part of Jesus' earthly ministry – it was. However, there were some times when he healed and some times when he didn't. Some may suggest that Jesus only stopped healing when there was no one to be healed. However, it is worth considering a number of times where this doesn't appear to be the case. On one occasion when Jesus was in Nazareth, he 'did not do many miracles there because of their lack of faith' (Matthew 13:58). It would also appear that although there were a 'great number of disabled people' (John 5:3) at the Pool of Siloam, Jesus only healed one paralysed man. Later, in Acts 3:1–10, we read about a man crippled from birth who was healed by Peter and John. Given that all the people 'recognised him', it seems inconceivable that Jesus had never passed him on his way in or out of Jerusalem. Lastly, it is seldom mentioned, but Jesus not only let Lazarus die[90], but also the two criminals with whom he was crucified. There were of course other occasions, such as in Luke 4:40, when Jesus *healed all* who were brought to him.

So what or who determined when Jesus would heal and who he would heal? Luke reminds us that 'the power of the Lord was present to heal the sick'. Given the 'power of the Lord' is unquestionably a reference to the Spirit, this is an incredible statement. Indeed it may even imply that there may have been times when the power of the Lord was *not* present to heal the sick. That of course is not to suggest that there was ever an occasion when the Spirit was absent from the life of Jesus. Rather, that there may have been times when his healing power was not made known through Jesus' ministry. Looking then at the breadth of the evidence, I would suggest that Jesus' healing ministry was determined by the guiding of the Spirit over and above the presence of the sick.

In that it clearly implies there may have been times when the power of the Lord was *not* with Jesus to heal those who were ill. Although again, a shock for many, I believe this is supported elsewhere.[91]

Secondly, 'the people all tried to touch him, because power was coming from him and healing them all' (Luke 6:19).

We have already looked at the enthralling story involving Jesus and the woman who had suffered with bleeding for twelve years.[92] However, here we witness an earlier incident in which *power* came out from Jesus. We know from Luke's gospel and the book of Acts that this word *power* is often used interchangeably with the Spirit. Luke tells us that people had travelled many miles to see and hear Jesus. Then, at some part of the day it was discovered that as they touched him people were being healed. Not one here and another one there. But all were being healed and becoming whole. I find it hard to imagine that the scene didn't start to resemble a rugby scrum as people rushed Jesus in utter desperation.

Having looked at these two passages, I believe we could fall into a dangerous trap. If we were not careful, we could see the Spirit solely as a *means to an end*. An impersonal force or remote power simply enabling Jesus to fulfil his goal. Yet nothing could be further from the truth. After healing a man who had been an invalid for thirty-eight years, Jesus makes the incredible statement 'Very truly I tell you, the Son can do nothing by himself; he can do only what he sees his Father doing, because whatever the Father does the Son also does (John 5:19).[93] I want you to grasp the magnitude of that. Jesus, who John has credited with Creation itself,[94] stated that he couldn't do anything by himself. Not that he wouldn't, but that he couldn't! I believe this beautifully reveals the relationship that Jesus had with the Father. Wherever he went and whatever he did, Jesus kept *an eye fixed* on heaven. His life was totally committed to bringing pleasure to the Father. Therefore, he couldn't and he wouldn't act independently from him, not even for a moment. This is so clearly demonstrated throughout the gospels. However busy or whatever demands people placed upon him, Jesus always prioritised prayer. I am sure it was through this living and loving relationship that the Spirit was given to him, *without measure.*[95]

THE SPIRIT WHO HEALS THROUGH US

A few years ago, I was invited by my great friend Sam Ward to speak at the Message's annual Eden Team Leaders' break. These incredible people live in some of the toughest areas in order to make Jesus known. Having prayed about what to speak on, my heart settled on successional leadership. I spoke again to Sam and together we agreed to buy a box of batons, usually used in a relay race. The plan was simple. At the end of our time, each person would be presented with a baton as a prophetic act. Our intention was to teach how we are called to pass on that which we have received. This act of passing on the baton can be seen throughout the Bible. We get a glimpse of it in the transition of leadership between Moses and Joshua, Elijah and Elisha, and Paul and Timothy. Then, in a very real sense between Jesus and his disciples, specifically in regard to healing. Let me explain. There is a moment in any relay race where two runners each have a hand on the baton. It is the time of change-over. During the latter part of Jesus' ministry, we witness this scenario. Although Jesus continued to heal in the power of the Spirit, he encouraged he disciples to do likewise. Jesus sent out the Twelve and then the Seventy-Two. On both occasions, he empowers them and commissions them to heal the sick.[96] Although there was a sense in which Jesus still ran beside them, the time would come, after his ascension, when they would be more fully released. Of course the disciples would never have been expected to run alone, but would continue in the power of the Spirit. Jesus therefore instructed that after his departure, they should wait in Jerusalem. Here he said they would 'receive power when the Holy Spirit comes on you' (Acts 1:8).

I encourage you to take the time to read through the Acts of the Apostles and marvel at the Acts of the Holy Spirit. You will see how time and again, God brought healing to the sick, through Jesus' flawed followers. You will witness Peter and John, healing the man crippled from birth at the Beautiful Gate (Acts 3:1–10); the Apostles healing many at Solomon's Colonnade (Acts 5:12–16); the previously unknown Ananias praying for Saul (soon to be Paul) to receive the restoration of his sight (Acts 9:10–19); Peter raising a man who had been bed-ridden for eight years (Acts 9:32–35); Paul saying 'on your feet' to a man who had been crippled from birth (Acts 14:8–10); and lastly, Paul healing Publius of fever and dysentery when shipwrecked on Malta. Given this incredible catalogue, it should be no surprise that when Paul wrote to his friends at Corinth he reminded them, 'My message and my preaching were not with wise and persuasive words, but with a demonstration of the Spirit's power' (1 Corinthians 2:4).

It was many years ago when I first discovered that the Bible was more than a history book which recorded God's supernatural activities of the past. It was also a guide, through which God wanted to shape my life and expectation. I am thankful that since then I have worshipped in churches that have been willing to pray for the seemingly impossible. I praise God, because over the years I have seen him work in remarkable ways and bring healing to many. However, if you still have doubts whether God intends to heal today, consider for a moment these three well-known passages. The Great Commission in Matthew's gospel records Jesus' final instructions to his disciples. Here he tells them to teach others 'to obey everything I have commanded you' (Matthew 28:20). Next, we come to the concluding verses of Mark's gospel. Here in Mark 16:9–19, Jesus assures his disciples that supernatural signs would follow those that believe. Although some early manuscripts don't include the text, there is of course no reason to believe that Jesus didn't speak these words. However, even if these words were added after Mark had concluded his script, the early church accepted them as consistent with both Jesus' teaching and their own experience. Then lastly, after the promise of the Spirit is fulfilled at Pentecost, Peter stands up to preach. In doing so, he shares how these events had been predicted hundreds of years before by the prophet Joel. God had said that in the last days, he would 'pour out his Spirit' (Acts 2:17–21). Some of the words that Peter quoted point us to the second coming of Jesus and are therefore still to be fulfilled. Therefore, it is safe to say that we still live in the last days. It is an age in which God has promised to move powerfully by his Spirit and a time in which we should expect to see and experience his healing power.

NO PLAN B

STEPPING OUT IN FAITH

On a number of occasions I have been privileged to preach at Grace Gospel Church in Bangalore, along with my good friend Bernard Thompson. The church is extraordinary for many reasons. Although their main meeting place is in essence a large a corrugated shelter, around six thousand gather every Sunday. Because the vast majority come from Hindu backgrounds, they have been very successful in planting many more churches in rural areas. When visiting, I have spent time asking church members how they have come to Christ. The consistency of their answers has been astonishing. Almost without exception they have described how they or a family member have been healed of a sickness or disease or delivered from a demon. One Sunday morning, Bernard and I shared the preaching at their five services. At the end of each service our dear friend, Pastor Samson Paul (whose father Rev. Dr. Arthur Paul had established the church), made an appeal. Samson simply asked that those wanting to receive healing should come forward. Each time, literally hundreds flocked to the front. The stewards faithfully served and tried to keep a semblance of order. However, only one thing was clear. Bernard would be responsible to pray for those at one side of the platform and I the other. I love to pray for people at the end of a service in our home church. If they are new or visiting, I like to introduce myself, ask their name and try to say something assuring. I then ask what they would like prayer for. Here, however, I was confronted with people simply pointing at parts of their body and stewards shouting, 'faster, faster'. My calculator tells me that two hundred people in twenty minutes accounts for a prayer every six seconds! In reality we couldn't go 'faster, faster'. Yet, despite being in a context I find uncomfortable and a culture that remains alien, the Spirit of God was working. Powerfully! I remember one lady, maybe in her late fifties, who had made her way forward, only to be overtaken by others. When a steward eventually spotted her she was brought towards me. Although able to walk, she seemed hesitant in her movement and quite fearful of the crowd. In the few seconds I had with her, I gently placed my hand upon her back. As I prayed I was aware that her bones began to move and her stoop began to straighten. In reality, I was not too sure who was most surprised, her or me! Although the language barrier and time restraints prevented much feedback, I do know that God's healing power was demonstrated at that moment.

Whenever I reflect on Grace Gospel Church (along with others that I have visited overseas), one thing strikes me. They perceive supernatural healing as normal and not exceptional. Of course it is possible that where there is no NHS or little provision for the poor, that God simply demonstrates exceptional mercy. It has also been suggested that in places of low literacy, God uses other means in order to point people to the Saviour. Although there may be some truth in both of these observations, the biggest difference I witness is one of expectation! Those who pray do so in faith and those who come forward, and continue to come, believe that God will meet their need.

I recently read Alan Scott's book, *Scattered Servants*. As I did, I was struck by his honesty as he shared his fear having been persuaded to pray for the sick on the streets by his close friend Mark Marx. Despite being the senior pastor of the fast growing Causeway Coast Vineyard Church, he acknowledges: 'The open secret – in most churches – is that we have a theology of healing, yet most people we pray for don't get healed. Moreover, we are somewhat surprised if they do.'[97] Alan goes on to reveal the incredible healings that they witnessed both inside and outside the church. Yet, the truth remains. We still do not see and experience all that we hope for. So how do we bridge the gap between what we read about in the Bible, throughout church history and overseas, against what we so often see and experience in our own lives? I am convinced that the answer may be as obvious as faith. The Bible speaks about faith in a number of different ways.

Firstly, there is Saving Faith. Paul writes to his friends in modern-day Turkey, 'For it is by grace you have been saved, through faith – and this is not from yourselves, it is the gift of God not by works, so that no one can boast' (Ephesians 2:8). In essence, Paul is saying that you and I offer nothing towards our salvation and even the faith that we exercise in God is a gift from him.

Secondly, there is what I will describe as Special Faith. In 1 Corinthians, Paul lists a number of supernatural gifts of the Holy Spirit. These include gifts of healing, prophecy, different kinds of tongues and faith.[98] This gift appears to be a unique and powerful expression of faith. I believe there are a number of times when God has given me this faith. On one occasion I had a phone call from a woman asking if her brother, a professing atheist, could come to see me. The moment I met this man in our church foyer, I knew I would lead him to Jesus within the hour. I didn't hope, or wish, or even pray, I knew. My conviction came simply because God gave me a gift of faith. Please don't misunderstand me. I don't live on that level all of the time, but there are occasions when God gives us that which we don't ordinarily possess.

Thirdly, there is what I call Sustaining (or enduring) Faith. This is the faith that you and I exercise day by day, from the moment we get up, to the moment we go to bed. It is an acknowledgment of God in the regular pattern of life. It is the type of faith that Paul calls 'faithfulness' (Galatians 5:22–23), when he lists the fruits of the Spirit in the life of a believer. I remain convinced that that it is here, in the everyday and the ordinary, that God wants us to believe that he will work extraordinarily, in and through our lives.

THREE SIMPLE SUGGESTIONS

A few weeks ago I bought a new contraption for the garden. It came disassembled. Looking at the few parts and a sheet of instructions, I thought it would take no more than five minutes to put together. Half an hour later, I was sorely tempted to throw it through the still-closed window! Given that (and other) bad experiences, I want to avoid instructions for instant success and instead highlight three simple suggestions.

1. Experience the Heart of the Father

I believe that if we are to be effectively used in healing ministry then we need to understand the heart of the Father. Jesus said to Nicodemus, 'For God so loved the world that he gave his one and only Son' (John 3:16). This love was the very catalyst of Jesus' mission. It was this love that Jesus revealed when he restored the leper and raised the little girl. Healing is intended to be a constant demonstration of God's love and power to a broken world. That of course is not to suggest that everyone will be healed all of the time. There have been occasions in the past where I have had to share with congregations why those we have prayed for, have not been healed. Although I still believe in the explanations I have given, I am convinced my belief in the sovereignty of God should not be an excuse for my lack of faith. We live in an age between the cross and the return of Christ, a time in which the kingdom has come, but the fullness of its power has not yet been revealed. Every miracle we witness reveals Jesus' triumph at Calvary. Every healing acts as a signpost which points to the restoration of God's glorious order. So let's be clear about this, we must not *shrink back*, but rather, *press on*. God's plan is that you and I act in faith in order to bring healing to the sick. [99]

2. Know the Authority of the Son

I believe that if we are to be used effectively in healing ministry then we need to understand the authority of the Son. Many years ago, I asked our youth leader, Chris, to pop to a local shop, in order to collect *some stuff*. As he was leaving, Chris realised that he had no money on him. The truth was, nor did I! Knowing the shop-keeper, I told Chris to go and to say, 'Gareth has sent me'. A few minutes later Chris returned, with a smile on his face and the two bags of shopping. There is a sense in which Chris had gone in my name and therefore received what he had asked for. This is what it means to go in the name of Jesus. It means that we can receive what we ask for, because of the authority of the one who has sent us. That is why in so many of the passages we referenced in Acts, we hear people healing the sick in 'the name of Jesus'. So be encouraged. As we step out in faith, we must do so with absolute confidence in the authority of Jesus' name.

3. Move in the Power of the Spirit

I believe that if we are to be effectively used in healing ministry then we need to understand the power of the Spirit.

As we know, there is *No Plan B!* If Jesus healed in the *power* of the Spirit, there is no way we could fulfil his mission alone. However, I do want to suggest that before we operate in the power of the Spirit, it's really helpful to get to know the person of the Spirit! Tracey and I have been married for over twenty-five years. There are times when I know what she is thinking and times I laugh because I know what she is about to say. Of course married life hasn't always looked like this, but the longer that we have been in one another's presence, the better we have got to each other. It is worth considering what we mean by the presence of the Spirit. Of course the Holy Spirit is ever present in time and space. However, it is my understanding and experience that the ever-present Spirit, still likes to *show up* somewhere. There was never a time where the Spirit was absent from the life of Jesus. Yet, we have read about the time that, 'the power of the Lord was with Jesus to heal those who were ill' (Luke 5:17). There will never be a time where the Spirit is absent from our lives. However, if we want to experience his power, we need to understand his person. We need to experience his felt and manifest presence.

EVERYDAY MINISTRY

A few years ago, I picked up my car from a local garage. As one mechanic finished the job, the other started to tell me about his own struggle and his wife's appalling illness. There are some occasions when I just listen and nod. But there are others when I know I must act. I explained that I was a Christian, believed that God loved him and asked if I could pray. I promised I wouldn't do anything weird and that his mate wouldn't even know that I was praying. I simply placed my hand on his shoulder as I would a friend. I then prayed something really simple and fairly brief. As I looked up, I could see tears welling up in his eyes. I only met Mark one more time. He was with a crowd of other mechanics, but made a point of coming over to speak to me. He quietly said, 'thank you, thank you, thank you'. I would love to know if Mark's wife was healed or whether their circumstances changed rapidly. However, I do know that Mark experienced the love of God and has now at least met one person who believes in a God who can heal.

One of the best things about understanding Jesus healed by the power of the Spirit is the discovery that we can follow his glorious example. I encourage you to pray and ask that God would use you in order to bring supernatural healing to others. I encourage you to spend time with God and become more sensitive to the leading of his Spirit. In doing so, I believe God will use you in order to transform the ordinary into the extraordinary!

CHAPTER EIGHT

OPPRESSED

'...to set the oppressed free' (Luke 4:18)

My first significant overseas trip was a mission visit to South America. Despite some of the memorable things I witnessed, it was one conversation that has lived with me the longest. I was walking round Rio de Janeiro, a city built in the most stunning of settings. Making our way through the colourful streets, I was attracted to a large crowd that had gathered in a nearby square. For a few minutes, I watched as a magician (and I use the word carefully) practiced his dark arts. Although always fascinated by those who, by sleight of hand, outwit their audiences, I had never witnessed anything quite so sinister. The show then progressed in the most appalling of ways. The magician singled out members of the audience, then one by one, placed curses upon their lives. You've guessed it. These curses could only be broken in exchange for money. I said to Paulo, the Brazilian pastor who was acting as our guide, 'you would never see anything like this back in the UK'. Paulo smiled as he replied, 'no, because all of your demons have stiff upper lips'. Looking back, I believe his comments had a bigger impact on me than the magician's display.

All of us have been raised in a country, society or community in which there was a predominant *worldview*. Our worldview acts like a lens through which we see and make sense of the world in which we live. Let me illustrate. I was born and raised in the UK and have therefore grown up in a culture that holds a predominately materialistic worldview. At school I was taught to believe in what I could see, what I could touch and in what I had experienced. I was encouraged to pursue rational explanations, based on quantifiable evidence and to call everything else into question. This worldview has some staggering shortfalls. Imagine for a moment, a frog in the bottom of a well. The frog is happy and safe. As long as flies come its way, it has enough to eat and through rain or condensation, enough to drink. Lastly, whether full or empty, the frog finds refuge in the brickwork of the well. Because the frog knows nothing other than the well, it assumes there is nothing beyond it. In some ways I believe my generation are like the proverbial frog in the well. However, there are countries and cultures, particularly in the non-Western world, which reject this materialistic worldview. Although not rejecting the physical, they are certainly more willing to embrace the spiritual. This may provide some explanation as to why Charismatic and Pentecostal Christianity is growing so quickly in these nations. However, it is important to realise that an openness to anything that is spiritual is just as dangerous as a rejection of everything that is spiritual.

I believe we would be naïve to assume that once we become Christians, we immediately lose the worldview with which we were raised. My good friend and pastoral colleague Chris Eke was born and raised in Ghana. Over the years, God has spoken to Chris in a number of amazing ways. Whenever Chris has a vivid dream, he immediately asks whether the Lord is speaking to him. Conversely, if I have a vivid dream, I immediately wonder if I had too much cheese the night before! Coming from Ghana, Chris' worldview has encouraged him to be open to the spiritual. Mine has taught me how to default to the physical. Although both of us are Christians, we both need to ensure that we view the world through a biblical and not a cultural determined lens. I pray as we continue to consider the ministry of Jesus that God would give us a biblical worldview in order that we would learn to live in the fullness of it.

So let's return to the story of Jesus in his hometown synagogue. As he read the words of Isaiah, Jesus made a series of pronouncements. We have already explored what Jesus meant by his promise to preach the good news to the poor, to free prisoners and to restore the sight of the blind. Now we come to his promise to 'release the oppressed'. This is the only statement from Jesus' manifesto which is not included in either the Hebrew or Greek texts of Isaiah 61:1–2.[100] Although we cannot be sure, it is probably taken from Isaiah 58:6. Here, we find God rebuking his people for getting their priorities wrong. God highlights how they observe the external practices of religion, such as feasts and sacrifices, whilst neglecting more important matters, such as exploitation and poverty. It appears that by quoting this passage, Jesus is intent on establishing a righteousness that religious observance could never deliver. Although 'freedom for prisoners' may have been a reference to God's people returning from exile, 'release for the oppressed' appears to point to Jesus' freeing of people from demonic powers. This is implied by the Greek word translated 'oppression' and is visibly demonstrated throughout Jesus' ministry. It is also fascinating to note that the word used to describe 'freedom' and 'release' is the same word. Elsewhere it is commonly used to describe the forgiveness of sins. As we see, the gospel places a priority on spiritual freedom, but reveals how physical healing and deliverance comes both as a consequence and evidence of it.

AN UNPLEASANT INTRODUCTION

Prior to me starting to write this book, I read again the accounts of the four gospels. In doing so, I was struck with the amount of spiritual conflict that followed Jesus' ministry. Wherever he went and whatever he did, Jesus was opposed, by leaders, authorities and demonic powers. Luke introduces us to Jesus' number one adversary. He writes: Jesus 'was led by the Spirit in the desert, where for forty days he was tempted by the devil' (Luke 4:1–13). I don't want to spend too much time looking at someone I'd rather not, but I think a brief introduction may be helpful.[101] The devil, unlike God, has not always existed. As a created being[102] he is subject to the supreme will of God.[103] Unlike God, the devil is not all-powerful, ever-present or all-knowing. Although we don't know the details, we do know that at some time in the past, the devil *fell*, or was *cast out* of heaven. At that time it appears he took with him around one-third of the angels.[104] Throughout the Bible the devil is known by various names and alluded to in different ways. However, he is most commonly referred to as 'the devil', meaning accuser, or 'Satan', meaning adversary. In many ways these two titles tell us a great deal about him and his activities. The *devil* and his army of fallen angels, or demons, are fierce in their opposition to God and the people of God. As the Bible reveals, they will use any means and go to any lengths in order to hinder the *good news that brings great joy.*

Anyone who takes an interest in current affairs will know that wars are ever present in the world. Only recently I heard a BBC reporter explaining how there were at least half a dozen conflicts taking place in one particular nation. In the same way there are at least four fronts of spiritual conflict. The first is the obvious battle between God and the devil.[105] Although this is a very real battle, we must not be conned into thinking that the sides are equal or the outcome uncertain. God is all-powerful and his victory is sure. In order to understand the ongoing battle, some have used the helpful parallel of World War II. On May 8, 1945, the Allies announced Victory in Europe (V.E. Day). All across the continent people celebrated because victory was assured. Elsewhere, however, hostilities continued. World War II wasn't completely over until the announcement of the Japanese surrender on the 15 August (V.J. Day), almost three months later. After V.E. Day the final victory was never in doubt, however casualties had continued.

The second front is between those angels who serve God and those who follow the devil.[106] Although the Bible gives us glimpses of this battle, it tends not to reveal too much detail. (For the record, I always think that we should be suspicious of those who seek to *fill in the blanks* and build ministries around their conclusions!) Thirdly, the battle between the devil, his demons and humanity. Like many battles the weapons and strategies are numerous. I am therefore convinced that many of the political structures, philosophies and ideologies that are used to govern and exert influence over us are expressions of the devil's schemes.[107] Fourthly, the battle that we are looking at here in which demons exert power, not over people generally, but over the lives of specific individuals.[108]

NO PLAN B

By looking at four encounters Jesus had with demons in Luke's gospel, I trust we will discover a little more about the work of demons and much more about Jesus' authority over them!

FOUR ENCOUNTERS

1. An untimely interruption (Luke 4:31–37)

Over the years I've had some interesting interruptions while I've been speaking. There have been the obligatory mobile phones, babies crying and fire alarms. Possibly the most memorable interruption, though, was when one old lady shouted out in a Sunday morning service, 'I wasn't asleep'. She was. I had seen her mouth open and listened to her snoring!

Immediately after launching his manifesto in Nazareth we find that Jesus travelled to the nearby town of Capernaum. Here, he had an incredible interruption while teaching on the Sabbath. Luke informs us: 'In the synagogue there was a man possessed by a demon, an impure spirit. He cried out at the top of his voice, 'Go away! What do you want with us, Jesus of Nazareth? Have you come to destroy us? I know who you are – the Holy One of God!' (vs 33–34)

The first thing to notice is the man with the demons attended the synagogue and not the local coven! The idea that demons are somehow excluded from places of worship (or indeed the lives of worshippers) may be comforting to some, but is hugely naïve. The New International Version tells us the man was 'possessed'. The term 'demon possession' is often used by Greek lexicons and translations in order to indicate what it means to be under the power of a demon in some way. The term was first popularised through the Authorised Version of 1611. However, I believe that it has become quite an unhelpful term due to its portrayal in many horror movies and popular fiction. Additionally, 'possession' is an imprecise term which may suggest either ownership or simply control. While recognising that there is a very real 'dominion of darkness' (Colossians 1:13); we must also remember demons are not rightful owners of anyone. Rather, they are imposters and deceivers! The New Testament describes a number of ways which a demonic spirit can exercise power over a person, from either the outside or within. Before we go on, it is worth taking a moment to look in a little more detail.

The first term, which historically has always been translated as 'demon possession', comes from the Greek word *daimonizomai*. Although it is only once used by Luke (in the next encounter we will look at), it is more common in the other three gospels.[109] On each occasion we see that the 'demonised' person has a demon which has entered them, dwell within them or is cast out (exorcised) from them. The other Greek terms *echein daimonion* (having a demon, used here in Luke 4:33) or *en pneumati akatharto* (with an unclean spirit) also seem to suggest the idea of indwelling.[110]

In contrast to demons indwelling a person, the New Testament also speaks of a more general external oppression through harassment, attack, or temptation. However, since these things can be the result of an internal or external demon it is sometimes unclear which is being referred to. For example in Acts 5:16 we read that those 'tormented by unclean spirits' were healed by the Apostles. This could be a reference to those who were tormented by either indwelling or external spirits.

Although I am not wanting to trivialise a serious subject it appears there is a sliding scale used to describe the influence of demons. In the most extreme cases, demons inhabit people's bodies. They act like intruders and squatters who have set up camp in someone else's house. At the other end of the scale, demons appear as local vandals who cause aggravation by smashing windows and slashing tyres. This may be the difference between what some have called *possession* and *oppression*. These terms may suggest something of the extent of a demon's control or influence. However, they do not determine the ways in which the control is manifest. For example Luke describes the actions of an evil spirit which caused a young boy to have seizures and another that enabled a slave girl to predict the future.

Coming back to the story. Did you notice that despite many of the people still being undecided about Jesus, the demon had no doubt about his identity? The demon knew Jesus of Nazareth was the Holy One of God. In response to this confession, Jesus didn't get into a conversation or enter a debate. He instructed the demon to 'be quiet' and to 'come out of him'. The fact 'the man was thrown to the ground' shows the power the demon had. However, the fact that the man was not injured may reveal the authority Jesus exercised in the situation. The demon was then sent packing!

2. The chain breaker (Luke 8:26–39)

Every town has its characters. Some may be eccentric, some a bit dodgy and others just downright dangerous. However, I don't suspect many towns have anyone to rival the man who Jesus encountered in the area of Gerasenes. The man lived in the local cemetery, wandered naked, and despite being shackled hand and foot, would break every chain and overpower any guard. On seeing Jesus, the man fell at his feet and bellowed, 'what do you want with me, Jesus Son of the most-high God?' In answer to the question: Jesus wanted everything to do with him and nothing to with the demons which tormented him. Jesus asked the man his name, to which he replied, 'Legion, because we are many'. If this demon was telling the truth, that's a startling fact. A Roman legion numbered six thousand men. Yet Jesus was anything but intimidated. He commanded the demons to leave the man but granted them permission to enter a herd of pigs. The pigs ran as fast as their trotters could carry them down the hill. They then dived like lemmings into that lake below. After a brief conversation, Jesus told the man, 'Return home and tell how much God has done for you'. Isn't that glorious? Only a few moments before, this man was an outcast to be avoided at all costs. However we see that Jesus not only released him from the demons which overpowered him, but immediately commissioned his as an evangelist! The man was entrusted with *good news that would bring great joy.*

3. 'My only child' (Luke 9:37–53)

The thing that any parent fears is watching their child suffer. I have listened on numerous occasions as parents have shared with me their stories and sobbed with sorrow. At other times, I have been summoned to hospitals and witnessed the fear etched upon their faces. In this story we see a desperate dad and his seriously ill son. Luke says, the day after Jesus' transfiguration,[111] he and his disciples came down the mountainside, where they were met by a large crowd. A father approached Jesus and described the situation concerning his 'only child'. He said that 'A spirit seizes him and he suddenly screams; it throws him into convulsions so that he foams at the mouth'. There are two things that I think are worth noting.

Firstly, let's look at this boy's affliction. It is often suggested that he suffered with epilepsy. The argument follows, in an age of limited medical knowledge, this and any other condition which was not understood were simply blamed on demons. In response, it is important to note a passage in Matthew's gospel. We read: 'News about him (Jesus) spread as far as Syria, and people soon began bringing to him all who were sick. And whatever their sickness or disease, or if they were demon possessed or epileptic or paralyzed—he healed them all' (Matthew 4:24). Here, Matthew makes a distinction between those afflicted by demons and those with epilepsy. For many years my own wife has been treated for epilepsy. We remain thankful that Tracey's condition is under control and trust God will continue to protect her. Over the years a handful of Christians have been quick to assume this physical condition must have a demonic cause. Sadly, I know others who struggle with anxiety, depression or other mental health struggles who have received similar responses. Every doctor now recognises that physical symptoms can be caused by a number of factors. These includ, physical, emotional, psychosomatic and stress-related ones. After reading the gospels, I believe we can add spiritual and demonic to that list. However, we would be just as unbiblical to believe all sickness is caused by demons as we would if we thought that no sickness was. We must then learn to discern the cause of a person's sickness as well as praying for their symptoms. Of course there is much benefit in developing good listening skills or basic counselling techniques.[112] However, in order to discern demonic influence we need to become tuned to the voice of the Holy Spirit. It appears Peter had spiritual insight when he *saw* through the pretence of Simon the Sorcerer. It is possible that John has this ability in mind when he encourages us to 'test the spirits to see whether they are from God' (1 John 4:1). Without doubt, Jesus had this ability in bucketloads as God anointed him 'with the Holy Spirit and power, and how he went around doing good and healing all who were under the power of the devil' (Acts 10:38).

Secondly, the man said to Jesus, 'I begged your disciples to drive it out, but they could not'. I bet the disciples hadn't passed this information on to Jesus! The two parallel accounts help us understand what lay behind the disciples' failure. In Matthew 17:14–21, Jesus suggests the disciples had insufficient faith. Then in Mark 9:14–29, he informed them, 'This kind (of demon) only come out with prayer', with some manuscripts adding, 'and fasting'. I am not going to suggest 'five simple steps to deliverance ministry'. However, if I did, I would put this advice high on the list. In order to reveal why, I want to remind you of the vivid story in Acts 19. Here we are introduced to the seven sons of Sceva, the High Priest. These brothers were all exorcists who one day had a bright idea. They started to use the name of Jesus in order to add a little weight to their ministry. Sadly for them, on one occasion the evil spirit answered, 'Jesus I know, and I know about Paul, but who are you?' (Acts 19:15). Then, the man with the spirit jumped up and gave them a good hiding. The brothers ran out of the house, naked, bruised and bleeding. Although there is no evidence that these brothers were true believers in Jesus, we do see an interesting parallel with Jesus' own disciples. I believe God wants us to understand the real authority that is invested in the name of Jesus. We will never learn that through reciting prayers or repeating formulas. Nor will we become more frightening to the enemy by shouting louder or by acting assertively. Rather, we discover our true authority as we study God's word and through times of prayer and even fasting.

4. The finger of God (Luke 11:14–26)

As we have discovered, some suggested Jesus drove out demons by the power of 'Beelzebub'. In response, Jesus reveals that he drove out 'demons by the finger of God'. Although Matthew records the same conversation, it is fascinating that he quotes Jesus saying he cast out demons 'by the Spirit of God' (Matthew 12:28). Either Matthew or Luke appear to substitute one term for the other and in doing allow us to understand the 'finger of God' and the 'Spirit of God' are interchangeable. So why does Luke not simply use Matthew's phrase in order to keep the conversation simple? In the book of Exodus the *finger or God* is used to write the Ten Commandments on tablets of stone.[113] Later, the Egyptian magicians used the phrase in order to explain how Moses performed miracles. Tragically for his people, however, Pharaoh's heart remained hard.[114] It is possible then that Luke is suggesting that Jesus wouldn't have been the first person who was rejected after performing miracles by the power of the Spirit. If this was the case I suspect it didn't go down well with Jesus' critics.

So, having disclosed the source of his power, Jesus reveals the consequence of his power. Because demons are cast out, the people could be 100% certain 'the kingdom of God has come to you'. Throughout the gospels, 'the kingdom' is the area over which the king exercises his rightful authority. Therefore, whenever Jesus entered a neighbourhood, we notice the demons get nervous. It seems they knew their dominance was about to be challenged.[115] I believe that this was true two thousand years ago and it is certainly true today. There may be resistance and there could be a fight. There will however only be one winner![116]

A WISE RESPONSE

I know this is embarrassing, but from time to time I find myself in the car listening to Radio 4's Woman's Hour. A couple of years ago, they broadcast a brilliant serialisation of C.S. Lewis' *The Screwtape Letters*. This book is a series of fictional letters between two devils; Screwtape, a senior devil, and Wormwood, his nephew and junior devil, whom he mentors. In the introduction Lewis makes this brilliant observation 'There are two equal and opposite errors into which our race can fall about the devils. One is to disbelieve in their existence. The other is to believe, and to feel an excessive and unhealthy interest in them. They themselves are equally pleased by both errors, and hail a materialist or a magician with the same delight'.[117] Although written in 1942, I think these two remain. So how should we respond to the demonic?

1. We should avoid denial

Do you remember the frog in the well? Just because we don't see something it doesn't mean it doesn't exist. Just because we have been raised as material rationalists doesn't mean we can dismiss the teaching of the Bible. Consider for a moment some of the issues we face in our society. The present prison population crisis, record rates of substance abuse, extreme gender politics, the appalling rise of racism and right-wing nationalism. Then consider members of your family and close friends who don't experience freedom, hope or release. Although we can attribute their struggles to 101 factors, I want to remind you of Jesus' words. He said, 'The thief comes only to steal and kill and destroy; I have come that they may have life, and have it to the full' (John 10:10). The bad news is of course that the devil hasn't changed. The good news is, nor has Jesus!

2. We should avoid obsession

Every church I have ever known has a fringe of people who blame the devil for their every struggle. Although I am not doubting we are in a spiritual battle, I don't believe the devil causes me to spill my coffee or encourages my neighbour's conifers to block out the light to my living room! I am convinced this sort of blame game is based on superstition more than it is on biblical understanding. However, as Lewis says, I am sure the devil still responds to it in sheer delight.

3. We should seek to adopt a biblical approach

So then... please read on!

THREE HOME TRUTHS

A few years ago Tracey and I experienced one of the toughest times in our lives. During that period I was coming to the end of a sermon series, based on Paul's letter to the Ephesians. I remember sitting down one morning in order to prepare my next message. I opened my laptop, read the text and stared at the blank screen for what seemed like hours. On the Saturday night I shared the situation with Tracey. The following day I was due to preach from Ephesians 6:10–13, in which Paul teaches we are in a spiritual battle and therefore need to wear spiritual armour. The problem was, I had no notes and no idea of what I would say. Having prayed together, I went away and in fifteen minutes prepared three PowerPoint slides, each revealing one of three points. I remember the next day that the church was full and the Holy Spirit worked powerfully. I also recall that I only really preached to two people. The first was Tracey and the second was myself! Praise God, however, that many others were also encouraged. I am thankful that God led us through that time and, through it, taught us things we may not have learned without it! I want to briefly share the three points with you.

1. We have a real enemy

If we are to effectively defend ourselves against the enemy, the more aware of his attacks we are, the safer we will be. Peter writes, 'Be self-controlled and alert. Your enemy the devil prowls around like a roaring lion looking for someone to devour' (1 Peter 5:8). A few months ago, I watched a TV documentary about a pride of lions in the Serengeti. When a herd of zebra wandered into their territory, you could almost see the lions lick their lips. It was obvious the lions were not going to attack a strong zebra in case it escaped and blew their cover. Instead, they waited until they identified a weaker zebra. As soon as the animal wandered away from its herd, the lions attacked. Moments later, dinner was served! It is essential believers remain together in order to defend themselves (and others) from the attacks of the enemy. Time and again I have seen Christians wander away from church in order to go it alone. Sadly, on all too many occasions, I have seen them attacked and overcome by the devil, in the same way that the zebra was killed by the lion.

2. We are in a real battle

Going back to the words of Paulo in Rio. I realise that no culture or country has a monopoly on the demonic. Although there has been a rise of occult activity in the West, I am aware that the devil's schemes can still be subtle. Consider for a moment the teenager from a dysfunctional home seeking recognition from the wrong crowd; or the wife who lives in fear of her abusive, but outwardly respectable husband; or the church leader with a secret porn addiction; or the committed Christian who has allowed a root of bitterness to become established in their life through unforgiveness. In one way or another, all these people have become casualties of war.

There are tried and tested ways by which the devil seeks to gain influence over a believer. The first is through temptation. Every day, we each face numerous temptations. These temptations prey on our fallen, sinful nature and seek to draw us from a dependence on God. Although it is not always the case, there are occasions when these temptations may come from a demonic source. This was certainly true with King David in the Old Testament and with Ananias in the New.[118] The next way by which the devil will seek to gain influence over our lives is by attacking us. This demonic opposition was very evident in the ministry of Jesus as well as in the book of Acts.[119] During our time in Manchester we were involved in church planting in a local housing estate in partnership with The Message. Although we talked openly with residents, local councillors and other church leaders, we soon discovered whatever we said was widely misunderstood. Some time later, a number of our Eden Team discovered occultic paraphernalia, including ceremonial knives, carefully hidden in their gardens. We were sure that we were in the battle which Paul referred to in Ephesians. A battle, not against 'flesh and blood', but 'against the powers of this dark world and against the spiritual forces of evil in the heavenly realms' (Ephesians 6:12). In light of this, we called the church to prayer. Although taking the threat seriously, we were reminded that every demon in hell is no match for the Lord Jesus. After the discovery and subsequent prayer, we came into a time of real breakthrough. Whatever battle you are facing right now, I want you to be encouraged through these wonderful words. John says 'The reason the Son of God appeared was to destroy the devil's work' (1 John 3:8).

An effective defence

There were numerous occasions when the Apostle Paul was slammed up as a political prisoner. However, Paul being Paul he didn't sit back and moan about his circumstances. He used his time for the glory of God. On one occasion, when imprisoned in Rome, it is likely that he would have been guarded closely (or even chained to) a Roman soldier. Paul, under the inspiration of the Spirit, had a great idea. He used his guard's armour as a metaphor by which he could teach about spiritual warfare. Paul speaks about the belt of truth, the breastplate of righteousness, feet ready to go with the gospel, the shield of faith, the helmet of salvation and the sword of the Spirit.[120] Whenever I read this passage I always notice how these items are primarily defensive. In any fight, an individual or even an army needs to master two skills. The first is defensive and the second is offensive. I believe that the same is true of Christians who find themselves caught in this battle between the kingdom of God and the dominion of darkness.

A forceful attack

A Roman soldier would carry two swords. The first was a large, heavy sword to be used in fierce battle. However, tucked into his belt he would also carry a small sword, called a *machaira*. This was designed to be effectively used in close combat. When Paul speaks about the sword of the Spirit, it is this sword which he refers to. Remember again the example of Jesus as he was tempted by the devil in the wilderness. Each time the devil put a temptation in his way, Jesus overcame as he proclaimed the truth of Scripture. Jesus effectively used the *sword of the Spirit*, the Word of God.[121]

3. We have a real victory

I want to remind you of some basic maths that is presented by James, the brother of Jesus. James writes, 'Submit yourselves, then, to God. Resist the devil, and he will flee from you' (James 4:7). That's brilliantly succinct. If all we do is submit to God, the devil will continue to lie in wait ready to pounce. If we try to resist him in our own strength, we will be quickly overcome. But in the same way one plus one always equals two, if we submit ourselves to God, and in his strength, resist, then the devil has no choice but to pack his bags and scarper!

I am convinced that as we continue to make Jesus known in a hostile world, we will face all kinds of demonic attack. We must remain alert and be aware of the devil's schemes. We must however, not be afraid. I am reminded of Jesus' response, when the

Seventy-Two returned after their first mission trip. They came to Jesus with much excitement saying, 'Lord, even the demons submit to us in your name.' Jesus response is revealing. He said, 'I saw Satan fall like lightning from heaven' (Luke 10:17–18). Without being disrespectful, it is possible that Jesus is having a flash-back to the time when the devil was cast from heaven at the beginning of time. However, given our understanding of Jesus' nature and the fact that Jesus speaks in the present tense, I believe this is unlikely. Instead I am convinced Jesus is speaking *symbolically*[122] as he sees the dominion of darkness give way to the kingdom of light! This wonderful observation should fill us with excitement and stir within us a greater confidence in the gospel.

Finally, I want to remind you of the illustration concerning V.E. Day. Although the battle continued, the victory was secure. The Apostle Paul reminds us how and where Jesus won his victory. He says:

> 'God made you alive with Christ. He forgave us all our sins, having cancelled the charge of our legal indebtedness, which stood against us and condemned us; he has taken it away, nailing it to the cross. And having disarmed the powers and authorities, he made a public spectacle of them, triumphing over them by the cross.' (Colossians 2:13–15)

The picture which Paul paints is of a Roman General returning from war. Having secured the victory, the crowds would flock in order to cheer his arrival. The General would head the procession, followed by his triumphant army. Then, at the back of the procession would follow the defeated army along with their generals, 'stripped of their dignity, rendered powerless, publically humiliated and held up to contempt'.[123] Paul is reminding us then of the glory, the wonder and the power of the cross.

It is through the cross that God has made his love known to us through the willing sacrifice of his son, the Lord Jesus. It is through the cross that justice is revealed and his forgiveness offered. It is through the cross that we have been brought into a living and loving relationship with our Heavenly Father. Therefore, because of the cross we can rejoice, 'because the one who is in you is greater than the one who is in the world' (1 John 4:4).

CHAPTER NINE

JUBILEE

'...to proclaim the year of the Lord's favour' (Luke 4:19)

I've finally got round to reading a book I first came across a few years ago. *The Year of Living Biblically* is a record of A.J. Jacobs' efforts to follow every instruction in the Bible for a whole year. A.J. is a secular Jew who lives in New York. Over a period of 365 days he met with parish priests, evangelical pastors, Amish representatives and local rabbis. In his desire to understand the Bible, A.J. becomes increasingly confused and hilariously hung up over the most ridiculous obscurities. Although he obsesses over each and every law, sadly A.J. doesn't appear to step back for long enough in order to understand the purpose of them.[124] After Israel left captivity in Egypt, God gave them numerous Laws through Moses. Although we often focus on the Ten Commandments, God gave over six hundred other instructions. These covered everything from family relationships, business practices, sexual purity and sanitary hygiene right through to dietary regulations. Through these Laws, God reveals his concern with every aspect of his people's lives. God also gave a calendar of events for Israel to follow. Firstly, there was the Weekly Sabbath. Once a week, every man, woman and child were to rest from their labours and set aside time for worship. Secondly, there were annual feasts and fasts. Although numerous, four are worthy of special mention. Passover, when the people celebrated deliverance from Egypt. Pentecost, when they remembered the giving of the Law. Tabernacles, through which they looked back to their wanderings in the desert as well as looking forward to the coming of Messiah. And lastly there was the most holy day in the Jewish calendar, The Day of Atonement. Thirdly, there was a timetable by which Israel could order their agriculture and economy. Every seven years there would be a Sabbath for the land in order that it would be left fallow. Then every seven Sabbaths, there would be an additional Sabbath, or Year of Jubilee.

There's little doubt Isaiah suggested that the coming Messiah would usher in the blessings of Jubilee.[125] So when, Jesus proclaimed 'the year of the Lord's favour' (Luke 4:19), the people knew what he meant and who he was claiming to be. The 'year of the Lord's favour' (sometimes translated 'the acceptable year of the Lord') was a direct reference to the Year of Jubilee.[126] But what exactly was this year and what was the significance for Jesus' ministry and what are the implications for us?

A FRESH LOOK AT JUBILEE

The Jubilee 2000 Coalition, endorsed by people as diverse as Muhammad Ali, George Carey and Thom Yorke, hit the media in 1999. The coalition had one goal, namely to wipe out the $90 billion debt owed by the world's poorest nations in the year 2000.

Although first devised in the early 1990's, the concept had its roots in the Old Testament concept of Jubilee. Although assessments of its success vary, billions were wiped off balance sheets and millions were helped. Those who remember the campaign may be tempted to impose its principles onto the biblical text. But if we really want to understand what Jesus was saying, we need to take a fresh look at Leviticus 25.

Let's start with Sabbath. God's plan was that when the Israelites were to give the ground one fallow year every seven. Because farmers acknowledge its benefits, many still rotate crops, use nutrients or leave alternate fields unploughed and unseeded to this day. As God placed a blanket ban on the Israelites from sowing their crops or tending their vines on the Sabbath Year, the people were forced to exercise faith in his provision. Further details are given for God's plans for the Sabbath Year in Deuteronomy. Here we find, 'Every creditor should cancel the loan he has made to his fellow Israelite or brother, because the Lord's time for cancelling debts has been proclaimed' (Deuteronomy 15:2)[127]

In practice this meant there would be no sowing or reaping for two whole years. For anyone responsible for feeding a family, this must have felt like frightening instruction. But listen to the promise. God said, 'I will send you such a blessing in the sixth year that the land will yield enough for three years. While you plant during the eighth year, you will eat from the old crop and will continue to eat from it until the harvest of the ninth year comes in' (Leviticus 25:21–22). That's extraordinary. God promises to provide abundantly for his people. Not for one, but for two fallow years. I believe it's important to remember that God continues to provide for his people today. Listen to how Paul encouraged his friends at Philippi. He said, 'And my God will meet all your needs according to the riches of his glory in Christ Jesus' (Philippians 4:19). I am sure that Paul's confidence came through both revelation and experience. Time and again, God had met his needs through supernatural means. As I look back over the last few years, I am staggered at how God has met our needs in the most remarkable ways. God has sometimes provided through prophetic words and on other occasions, extraordinary circumstances. However, as I look ahead, I remain convinced that God will provide, just as he promised to Israel.

Now we come to Jubilee. As we have seen every seven Sabbath Years (49 years), there would be the Year of Jubilee.[128] During the Year of Jubilee, three things happened. Ancestral land would be returned, debts would be written off[129] and slaves would be released. I believe these headlines all require a little more understanding.

Firstly, ancestral land would be restored. God knew that however the land was allocated, much of it would change hands over fifty years. Those who prospered would have *bought up* and those who were struggling would have *sold up*. In reality, the rich would have got richer and the poor would have got poorer. Therefore, God established the Year of Jubilee in order that all the families could make fresh starts. In light of this, the land was never really sold, only ever leased. In fact, God said its price should be determined, whether high or low, by the number of years to Jubilee 'because what is really being sold to you is the number of crops' (Leviticus 25:16). Through this system, God encouraged the entrepreneur while protecting the vulnerable. God's purpose was clear. The land was not the people's to sell, because God said, 'the land is mine and you are but aliens and my tenants' (Leviticus 25:23).

Secondly, debts would be written off. The Bible teaches us a lot about money and our responsibility towards with it. Therefore, it is important to understand that nobody should borrow beyond the means that they expect to repay. It is also important that within a fair economy, lenders should not loan more than people can be reasonably be expected to repay. Therefore, by legislating that debts needed to be written off every seven years, God provided not only potential relief to debtors, but restraint to lenders. I believe God's heart for a just and compassionate economy can be clearly seen as he instructs the people how they should act towards the poor. God says, 'you must not lend (him) money at interest[130] or sell him food at profit. I am the LORD your God who brought you out of Egypt to give you the land of Canaan and to be your God' (Leviticus 25:38). Did you notice that? The basis of the people's kindness to the poor was in response to God's mercy towards them. In the same way, Matthew tells us when Jesus commissions his twelve disciples, he said, 'Heal the sick, raise the dead, cleanse those who have leprosy, drive out demons. Freely you have received; freely give' (Matthew 10:8). The basis of our mission, is to give to share with others the *good news* that has been given to us.

Thirdly, slaves would be released. Now it's important to recognise that this slavery was not the same as Afro-American slavery. Nor was it the equivalent of modern-day slavery, tragically so common in our society. However, in Israel there was provision that, if an Israelite became poor or destitute they could sell themselves into slavery.[131] However, just like foreign slaves, they could redeem themselves at any time. In order that people didn't find themselves in permanent slavery, God said, 'Even if someone is not redeemed in any of these ways, they and their children are to be released in the Year of Jubilee, for the Israelites belong to me as servants. They are my servants, whom I brought out of Egypt. I am the Lord your God' (Leviticus 25:54–55). Again, the basis of mercy in Israel was simple. God's people were called to be merciful in light of his mercy towards them.

SOUND THE SHOFAR

Every year three thousand people gather in our local market square in order to commemorate Armistice Day. Our local RAF squadron march, dignitaries lay wreaths and service aircraft fly over. At the end of a two-minute silence a lone bugle sounds the Last Post. Over the years the bugle has become synonymous with the Last Post and the Last Post with the bugle. The same was true in Israel with Jubilee and the ram's horn or *shofar*. The word Jubilee is even derived from the name given to this unique instrument. In Leviticus, God had decreed that on the Year of Jubilee, the people should 'sound the trumpet (or shofar) everywhere on the tenth day of the seven month; on the Day of Atonement' (Leviticus 25:9). Just like the Last Post this sound would be inseparable with a specific event. It was the sound of Jubilee. In light of that, let's return to Jesus. Here in the back-water of Nazareth, Jesus declared that he was anointed 'to proclaim the year of the Lord's favour' (Luke 4:19). I may have a vivid imagination, but as I picture the scene in the synagogue, I can almost hear the shofar sound!

In recent years I have become aware that many Christians simply skip over the Law of Moses. For various reasons they have concluded that it doesn't really apply to them and therefore they have little or no interest in it. Although we don't have time to explore this theme in any real detail, I just want to outline three reflections as to why The Law matters.

THREE REFLECTIONS

Firstly, as we have already seen, the Law teaches us about God's interest in the whole of his people's lives. I am not suggesting that we should try to follow the whole Law of Moses. So rest assured, I am not saying we should avoid wearing clothes of mixed fibres[132] or that we should skip bacon butties![133] However, we must understand that God is still concerned about what we wear and what we eat. In fact he remains interested in every aspect of our lives and continues to instruct us in holiness.

Secondly, the Law reveals our need of a Saviour. Those of us who are parents know we have the responsibility to teach our children right and wrong. In the same way, the Law highlights righteousness and sinfulness. The problem is, when we tell our children not to do something, we inadvertently plant in them a desire to do it. In Romans 7, the Apostle Paul teaches that the Law provokes a similar response in us and in in doing so highlights our inherent sinful nature. There was a common practice within Roman households whereby a father would appoint his son a tutor.[134] This legally appointed overseer would be charged to train and discipline a child in order to bring them to maturity. Paul says, 'The law was our guardian until Christ came; it protected us until we could be made right with God through faith' (Galatians 3:24). The purpose of the Law was to highlight and curtail our wrong, before leading us to righteousness in Jesus.

Thirdly, the Law leads us to Jesus. The tragic thing is that many people still try to win the favour of God by observing either the Law of Moses or another law that they have substituted for it. Let's see how ridiculous that is. Prior to meeting Jesus on the Damascus Road,[135] the Apostle Paul was a leading light in Judaism. Everything a devout Jew could want to be, Paul was. Everything a devout Jew should do, Paul did. But then, his life was turned upside down and back to front by Jesus. Later, Paul would reflect on the things that other admired about him. He said, 'I consider them garbage, that I may gain Christ and be found in him, not having a righteousness of my own that comes from the law, but that which is through faith in Christ – the righteousness that comes from God on the basis of faith' (Philippians 3:8b–9). This recognition that the Law was insufficient to save us is consistently taught through Paul's letters. Although Paul was never one to beat about the bush, he reserves his sternest words for the legalists at Galatia. Paul wrote, 'I do not treat the grace of God as meaningless. For if keeping the law could make us right with God, then there was no need for Christ to die' (Galatians 2:21). Then Paul asked them a question in order to underline his point. He said, 'I would like to learn just one thing from you: did you receive the Spirit by the works of the law, or by believing what you heard?' Galatians 3:2). The answer of course was obvious. The Galatians knew that they couldn't be saved, nor receive the Spirit through observing the Law.[136] The same of course is true for you and me. The observance of laws cannot save us, nor secure us the Spirit. We need the grace of God for both these things!

JUBILEE

FULFILLED

On one occasion, Jesus told the religious leaders of his day, 'If you really believed Moses, you would believe me, because he wrote about me' (John 5:46).[137] I assure you, if you were to read and reread the five books of Moses you will discover that Jesus of Nazareth isn't mentioned by name. That of course is not to suggest that he is not present. So what is Jesus saying? He is revealing how every Law and every sacrifice ultimately finds its true fulfilment in him.[138] Therefore, not only did Jesus honour the teaching of the Law, he also fulfilled the spirit for which it was given. This is so clearly seen when Jesus continued to heal people on the Sabbath, despite the protests of the religious police! [139]

Let me briefly explain a number of ways that we see the Old Testament fulfilled in the New, by referring to the major feasts that we mentioned earlier. It was during the feast of Passover, that Jesus was crucified.[140] As the *paschal lamb* had been slaughtered in order to bring deliverance to Israel, so Jesus becomes 'our Passover lamb' (1 Corinthians 5:7). Through the means of this insightful statement we see how it is through Christ alone that we find both deliverance and freedom. Next, we come to Pentecost when the Jews remembered the giving of the Law. You may recall that when Moses descended Mount Sinai having received the Ten Commandments, he witnessed how in his absence the people had turned to worship a golden calf. As a consequence the Levites drew their swords and 'about three thousand of the people died' (Exodus 32:28). Yet it was on this day that the Spirit was poured out upon the early followers of Jesus. At the end of Peter's preach, someone took the time to take a head count and reported 'and about three thousand were added to their number that day' (Acts 2:41). Praise

God because we later read, 'the letter kills, but the Spirit gives life' (2 Corinthians 3:6). By way of a quick reflection, in my experience this is an enduring principle. Sadly I have witnessed churches that are all but dead as a consequence of legalism. Lastly, we come to the Feast of Tabernacles, when the Jewish people looked forward to the coming of Messiah. Immediately preceding this feast was the Day of Atonement. Remember, according to Leviticus 25:9, it was on this day that the trumpet would sound and that Jubilee would be proclaimed throughout the land. I find that remarkable. Through his death on the cross, Jesus made atonement for our sins.[141] In doing so he was able to sound the start of the greatest Jubilee that anyone could ever imagine.

So, given our three reflections and the fulfilments that we have just witnessed, how should you and I relate to The Law? I am often reminded Jesus was once asked by a teacher of the Law, which was the greatest commandment? He answered 'Love the Lord your God with all your heart and with all your soul and with all your mind. This is the first and greatest commandment. And the second is like it: Love your neighbour as yourself.' (Matthew 22:37–40). I don't know about you, but I find it really difficult to do either of these. Therefore, the long and short of it is, I need the Spirit.

On one occasion Jesus said about his Heavenly Father, 'I always do what pleases him' (John 8:29). That's an incredible statement and one that we would want to echo. Yet, the only way I know I can is with the help of his Spirit. Some Christians of course are fearful of this teaching. They believe that it may somehow lead us to lawlessness or worse. However, in my weakness, I recognise that if Jesus depended on the Spirit, so must I. The only way I can accomplish God's ends is through his means. I must rely on his Spirit in order to live as he calls me to live. However, it is well worth remembering that Jesus' standards are not lower than the Law of Moses, they are higher. As Jesus famously said, 'You have heard that it was said, "You shall not commit adultery." But I tell you that anyone who looks at a woman lustfully has already committed adultery with her in his heart' (Matthew 5:27–28). Again, I need the Spirit, not in order that I can do what I want, but so that I can be empowered to do what God wants!

Let me remind you of Paul's summary to the church in Galatia. He writes, 'So I say, live by the Spirit, and you will not gratify the desires of the flesh. For the flesh desires what is contrary to the Spirit, and the Spirit what is contrary to the flesh. They are in conflict with each other, so that you are not to do whatever you want. But if you are led by the Spirit, you are not under the law' (Galatians 5:16–18).[142]

REASONS TO REJOICE

I am thrilled to play a small part in our local Christians Against Poverty (CAP) Debt Centre. A few weeks ago, I bumped into Steve and Angie who were among our first clients. When I first met this couple, they were anxious and isolated, their debts a consequence of poor decisions and exploitation. Through the love of the CAP team this couple have now come to Jesus and are part of a loving church family. Steve and Angie stopped excitedly to tell me how they had stuck to their management plan and in a matter of weeks would be debt-free. Better still, they and their church were having a party to celebrate. I walked away thrilled. Knowing something about their story, I am aware of the massive investment that the CAP team and the church have made into this couple's life. I also know how CAP headquarters negotiated with creditors in order to remove the pressure of dealing with the creditors directly and produced the financial plan that made all this possible. So in a sense, the celebration would be one to honour the staff and volunteers of CAP along with Steve and Angie for their hard work. This is what an Old Testament Jubilee celebration might have looked like – just on a national scale. It would have been a celebration of God's provision and people's obedience to it. Jesus' Jubilee, however, goes way, way beyond this. Sadly, over the years some have sought to simply politicise Jesus' proclamation of Jubilee. One commentator helpfully said, however, 'Jesus is no social reformer and does not address himself in any fundamental way to the political structures of this world, but he is deeply concerned with the literal, physical needs of men as with their directly spiritual needs'.[143] I think that is so important to understand. Jesus cannot be placed in a political straitjacket. Nor can he be accused of being so spiritual that he is of no practical help. Jesus is interested in our wellbeing: spiritually, physically, immediately and eternally!

So Jesus' Jubilee means that ancestral land will be returned. Whenever I read Genesis 1 and 2, I am shocked to see how people have been robbed of intimacy with God through sin. However through Jesus' love and righteousness we find that relationship may be restored and inheritance guaranteed. We also discover that that spiritual indebtedness which resulted from our sin and rebellion is forgiven. However, we need to remember that through the means of his death, Jesus didn't only address our deficit. Jesus takes us into surplus![144] Then, slaves are still set free from sin and its consequences in order to enjoy life and liberty in Jesus.

Lastly, think for a moment about what Jubilee celebrations would have looked like if Old Testament Israel had ever observed it. Then think about Steve and Angie's church celebration to give thanks for them being debt-free. Given what God has done for us in Jesus, I think it's fair to say we should be a partying people. I don't mean that in a flippant way. I know that Scripture speaks a lot about suffering and that Jesus calls us to take up our cross daily in order to follow him.[145] I am fully aware that we are called to alleviate suffering and go to the ends of the earth. However, it is better by far if we at least follow with a spring in our step and a smile on our face!

CHAPTER TEN

THE TWIST IN THE TALE

'All the people in the synagogue were furious when they
heard this.' (Luke 4:28)

Over the years, translators and publishers have developed a habit
of inserting titles into the biblical text. Given the majority of our
time has been spent looking at the Nazareth Manifesto, I want you
to turn to Luke Chapter 4 one last time. There, at the beginning
of the chapter you will find a heading. Although this may vary
depending on your translation, the vast majority announce: *Jesus
Rejected at Nazareth*. Given what we have explored, this may seem
an unexpected title. It is if you like, the twist in the tale. Despite
Jesus declaring that he would bring good news, free prisoners,
restore sight, release the oppressed and proclaim Jubilee, much
of the town still turned against him. Although that may sound
shocking to us, it wasn't a shock to God and nor did it derail the
mission of Jesus. If we are determined to live as Jesus' followers, it
is vital we understand some of the reasons why the people rejected
him and consider what the implications are for us.

Over the last thirty years I have preached most weeks, in possibly hundreds of churches. Given my experience, I am aware how different congregations will respond to my message in a variety of ways. There are times I have known a message has hit home and has been taken to heart. On other occasions, it has been received with a deafening silence! I have never, however, faced the response that Jesus received. Having read the scroll, Jesus handed it back to the attendant at the synagogue and started to speak. At the end of his message, Luke informs us, 'Everyone spoke well of him and was amazed by the gracious words that came from his lips' (Luke 4:22). I am sure when Luke says 'everyone', he means everyone. There was no split decision, nor heated debate, only unanimous agreement. Jesus had amazed the congregation through his gracious words. However, in what seems like a matter of moments, the crowd were trying to kill him. So what did Jesus say that had the same effect as lighting the blue touch paper?

What I'm about to say will generate some comments in my own church, but here goes: Jesus was a Northerner! As we say, Jesus called a spade a spade! Throughout his ministry he maintained the practice of telling people what they needed to hear, not what they wanted to hear. Therefore, the moment he received their praise, Jesus revealed just how superficial it was. Jesus challenged the crowd by saying, 'surely you will quote this proverb to me: Physician, heal yourself.' Jesus knew their thoughts. He knew they appreciated his talk, but were wondering whether he could walk the walk. Jesus knew the people were privately hoping he would do in Nazareth the miracles he performed in Capernaum. Worse however was still to come. Jesus reminded them of an event that took place in Elijah's time. It happened when God called Elijah to serve a Gentile widow and not a Jewish one. In the same way, Jesus reminded them that Elisha was used to heal a Syrian of leprosy, rather than one from among their own people. In a flash, the people turned against him. Forget his gracious words, the people now wanted his blood. They therefore drove him out of town to the brow of a hill. Anyone who has visited Nazareth will know the cliffs they sought to throw him off still remain. 'But Jesus walked right through the crowd and went on his way' (Luke 4:28).

THE CALL

So why, having longed for the coming of the Messiah, did the people reject Jesus so quickly? Why, in a moment did they shift from glad acceptance to violent rejection? In short, it's evident that Jesus wasn't the Messiah they were looking for! All four gospels make it clear that there was a chasm between the hopes of the people and the promises of Jesus. On this occasion the people appeared to reject Jesus on the basis of a single issue. They wanted a Messiah who would exclusively serve the Jewish nation. However, Jesus' words made it clear that his purpose was to reveal God's purpose to both Jew and Gentile. On other occasions, it appears the people wanted a Messiah who would lead an army in order to restore their national boundaries. However, Jesus made it clear he had come to inaugurate a spiritual kingdom. They wanted a Messiah who would do their will. But Jesus let it be known… he had come to do the will of God!

Over the years I have not only talked to people about Jesus, but have listened as they have expressed their opinion about him. Through this process I have discovered that not much has changed in two thousand years. People still attempt to mould Jesus according to their own personal preferences. However, the fact remains, Jesus is 'the same yesterday, today and forever' (Hebrews 13:8). In light of this, let's be reminded of the real words of the real Jesus. In Luke 9:18–27, we read the account of a revealing conversation between Jesus and his disciples. This took place at the beginning of his final year of his public ministry, around eighteen months after he had gathered the twelve around him. Although having been initially rejected at Nazareth, there had followed a season of relative popularity. However, for many the same problem remained. Jesus continued in his refusal to match their hopes and dreams!

The scene then is set at Caesarea Philippi, the source of the River Jordan. High above the gentle spring towered cliffs in which people had placed idols of Roman and Greek gods. In the shade of this pseudo-temple, Jesus asked his followers, 'Who do the crowds say that I am?' In response they listed the great and the good whom others had confused with Jesus. However, Jesus' enquiry was only a warm-up. The real question was still to come. 'But what about you?' he asked. 'Who do you say I am?' Peter's answer was short, but true. 'The Christ, the Son of God', he said. Having spent time with Jesus, having heard the teaching and seen the miracles, Peter was in no shadow of doubt. Jesus, he said, was the promised Messiah.

Immediately after this Jesus made one of his most startling statements. He said, 'whoever wants to be my disciple must deny themselves and take up their cross daily and follow me' (Luke 9:23). For centuries these words of Jesus have challenged all who have heard them. I believe this may be truer today than at any other time in history. We live in an age of gender fluidity and self-realisation. An age in which advertisers encourage consumers to spend money they don't have on stuff they don't need, just 'because you're worth it'. But the call of Jesus continues to be a call to deny oneself in order to gain something of greater worth. Although this may be difficult, it is not unreasonable. Any student studying for their finals and every athlete training for competition knows the importance of sacrifice. So it is for Jesus' disciples. Like our master, we must learn to pray 'not my will, but yours be done' (Luke 22:42) and in doing so prioritise eternal glory over immediate comfort.

Those in Western democracies were shocked to hear news of beheadings and crucifixions emerging from the so called Islamic State. But, two thousand years ago the sight of a condemned man[146] carrying a cross-beam was not uncommon. Having already been beaten and flogged, the man already half dead would be led slowly to his place of execution. Here, he would be stripped naked by his guards and nailed to the wood that he carried. The cross would then be raised to a vertical position and stand for as long as it would take the man to die. Sometimes a matter of hours, but more often a number of days. Although I could go on, the point is clear. Jesus instructs his disciples to renounce the right to life itself! For some (and according to church history, ten of the original twelve disciples), following Jesus would result in literal martyrdom. For all disciples, however, obedience to Christ intrinsically involves death. When Paul wrote to the Colossians he urged them, 'Put to death, therefore, whatever belongs to your earthly nature: sexual immorality, impurity, lust, evil desires and greed, which is idolatry' (Colossians 3:5). I don't believe Paul is speaking about an isolated incident, but an ongoing process. He refers to a lifestyle in which the disciple must take up their cross, not once, or twice, but as Jesus said, *daily*. Only moments ago, I received a notification that someone I have never heard of, from somewhere I don't know, is now following me on social media. When Jesus called us to follow him, he wasn't inviting us to have a passing interest in him. He was asking that we pursue him. Jesus gives us the privilege to continue his work on earth, to be inextricably associated with him, both in life and in death.

EXCITING EXPECTATIONS

The reason I have spent time commenting on Jesus' rejection at Nazareth is because it is so intrinsic to the story. The reason I have spent time commenting on Jesus' call to follow is because it is central to our story. I trust then we are under no illusions. However good the good news is, some will continue to reject it. They will refuse Jesus and those who follow him. So, let's not be deluded. The road ahead may be exciting, but it remains narrow[147] and will undoubtedly be rocky! However, as we have seen, both in the gospels and the book of Acts, many others will accept the gospel. As a consequence not only will they be transformed, but they will be used by God to bring transformation to others.

I love the way that Dr Luke begins the sequel to his gospel. He says, 'In my former book, Theophilus, I wrote about all that Jesus began to do and to teach until the day he was taken up to heaven, after giving instructions through the Holy Spirit to the apostles he had chosen' (Acts 1:2). As we have seen, the verse implies that the disciples will continue the ministry of Jesus. The point is explicitly demonstrated as the story of the early church unfolds. So given what we have discovered, how do we continue to see the greatest manifesto of all time, made known through our lives and in our generation? I believe we need to be committed to three things:

THE TWIST IN THE TALE

1. To the powerful and life-changing message of the gospel

As we have seen, over the years some have sought to redefine the gospel. In doing so, they have often settled on a message that is unrecognisable from the one the early church proclaimed. A message that is polite, inoffensive and in reality, powerless. A message that has been shaped by society and one therefore that is unable to transform it. A message in which the *offence* of the cross has been conveniently air-brushed out! The true gospel of course has always been perceived as a stumbling block to some and folly to others. However, we must be reminded that the foolishness of God remains wiser than human wisdom, and the weakness of God stronger than human strength.[148] That of course does not excuse those who act as stumbling blocks or who speak unwisely. In the day and age in which we live, it is essential that we speak the *truth* and where possible, the *whole truth* and *nothing but the truth*. We must, however, always do so with gentleness and respect.[149] I believe that failure to operate within this framework will simply result in the *good news that brings great joy* never being heard.

2. To the supernatural confirmation of the gospel

As we faithfully make known the truth about Jesus, we should expect for God to confirm his word with supernatural signs of healing and deliverance. One scholar insightfully commented that the miracles of Jesus were 'the audio-visual of God's power at work'.[150] That's a brilliant observation. However, God knows we need more 'audio-visuals'. I remain convinced that in the 21st-century Western world, healing and deliverance should not be seen as an add-on, an extra, or an option for some. Time and again, I am seeing God work miraculously in the lives of unbelievers who are seeking truth. These signs and wonders are used by God in order to evidence both the truth of the message and reveal to them his love. Over the years I have heard many people calling for balance in our appreciation of God's word and experience of his Spirit. Although I appreciate their heart, I believe their argument to be nonsense. I want you to imagine two children on either end of a see-saw. Although the scene may appear to be a happy one, in essence the two children are fighting for supremacy at either side of a fulcrum. The idea that the Word and the Spirit are two forces which need to be positioned in such a way to create harmony is deeply wrong. The Scriptures, which are breathed by the Spirit,[151] teach us how to walk with the Spirit. As we do so, the Spirit leads us, back to the very Scriptures which testify to Jesus. We don't therefore need a little less of either the Word or the Spirit in order to accommodate the other. We need more of the Word and more of the Spirit!

3. **To revealing the gospel known through
    social action and acts of compassion.**

Jesus didn't call us to be nominal, cultural or *box-ticking* believers, he called us to be cross-carrying disciples who would always be willing to follow. So, having looked at the sacrificial love of Jesus, I find it impossible to imagine a truly worshipping church unwilling to roll up their sleeves and get their hands dirty. Although there are some who would suggest that the church in the UK is becoming marginalised, we must be reminded of all that the church is involved in. Together we are the most significant providers of pre-school care, the largest employers of youth workers and provide the largest debt management service in the country. Long after austerity is officially over, I believe Christian-led food banks will continue to feed the hungry and Street Pastors will still patrol our towns and cities.

As I write I am acutely aware that there is a danger even in the categories that I present. For example, I want to mention the work of The Message and the fact that Eden is one of the largest missionary movements to the poor since the birth of the Salvation Army. My problem, however, is not knowing exactly how to label it. Is it a movement committed to the powerful and life-changing message of the gospel? Is it a movement committed to making the gospel known through supernatural means? Or, is it a movement committed to making the gospel known through social action and acts of compassion? The answer of course should be yes to all three. So it was with Jesus' manifesto and so it should be with our ministries. God does not call us to either one or another of these expressions of his love, he calls us to embrace them all.

A DAY OF OPPORTUNITY

We earlier discovered that Jesus appeared to read Isaiah 61 in part and not in whole. In fact it seems that he placed a full-stop midway through a sentence. The original text stated, 'to proclaim the year of the LORD's favour and the day of vengeance of our God' (Isaiah 61:2a). However Jesus proclaims the former and omits the later. He inaugurated Jubilee, but has reserved judgement until he returns. We find ourselves then between these two events. We live in the year of his favour. We live in the last days in which the Spirit continues to be poured out. But things will not continue like this forever. One day God will bring them to a sudden end. So then, between now and then, however long or however short, we live in a God-given time of opportunity.[152]

Therefore in light of this, we must always remember, there is *No Plan B!*

APPENDIX

I know it may be clichéd, but I was raised in a church that appeared to honour God the Father, God the Son and God the Holy Scriptures. It was acknowledged that the Spirit brought conviction of sin, was essential for new birth and was active in making us more like Jesus. However, the idea that the Spirit anointed Jesus, and now wanted to anoint us, would have been anathema to many. Furthermore, it was clearly stated that the supernatural manifestations and gifts of the Holy Spirit had ceased a few years after the death of Jesus.

Let me illustrate one of the many flaws of this position. At the end of Matthew's gospel we read what is often known as the Great Commission. Jesus said, 'All authority in heaven and on earth has been given to me. Therefore go and make disciples of all nations, baptising them in the name of the Father and of the Son and of the Holy Spirit, and teaching them to obey everything I have commanded you. And surely I am with you always, to the very end of the age' (Matthew 28:18-20). Firstly, please notice the disciples were told to instruct others to do the same as they had been commanded. Now I don't think that you need a sky-high IQ to realise that this must include healing the sick and casting out demons. Jesus didn't say 'teach most of the things I have instructed you', or 'everything apart from the supernatural stuff'. Jesus said, 'teach them to obey everything I have commanded you'! Secondly, Jesus promised to be with his followers, 'to the very end of the age'. That must have sounded reassuring to the disciples. The problem was that only a few days later Jesus was gone. So was this nothing more than a well-meaning promise that Jesus failed to keep? Absolutely not. Jesus had already told them that after he departed the Spirit would come. John reminds us that Jesus promised 'another advocate' (John 14:16). That means not only is Jesus our helper, but the Spirit is. The Spirit is *another* just like Jesus. Not another who comes as a second-rate substitute, but another of the same substance, character and nature.

At the age of seventeen I started to get serious with God. Through my own study and conversations, I became convinced I was being short-changed. I believed the Scriptures quoted to evidence that I shouldn't experience anything more of the Spirit actually indicated the opposite. It certainly appeared that those who accused others of being led by experience were being dictated to through fear and their own lack of experience concerning the work of the Spirit. As a consequence, I am thankful that God in his grace determined to fill me with his Spirit as a teenager. Although I am aware of the very many mistakes I have made since, none of these make me doubt the work of the Spirit. Rather, they serve to make me recognise my ongoing need of him and my need to be continually filled.

It's possible that you have never experienced the powerful work of the Spirit in your life. It's also possible that you have, but desire more. Whatever your situation, I want to share with you the following encouragement. After teaching his disciples about prayer, Jesus continues:

APPENDIX

'So I say to you: ask and it will be given to you; seek and you will find; knock and the door will be opened to you. For everyone who asks receives; the one who seeks finds; and to the one who knocks, the door will be opened. Which of you fathers, if your son asks for a fish, will give him a snake instead? Or if he asks for an egg, will give him a scorpion? If you then, though you are evil, know how to give good gifts to your children, how much more will your Father in heaven give the Holy Spirit to those who ask him!' (Luke 11:-12)

Isn't that glorious? I encourage you then, ask, seek and knock![153]

NOTES

CHAPTER ONE: THE LAUNCH

1   All Bible verses quoted are taken from New International Version (UK) unless otherwise stated

2   Matthew 3:13–17; Mark 1:9–11; Luke 3:31; John 1:29–33

3   Matthew 3:18–22; Mark 1:16–20. It is worth noting that although Matthew and Luke indicate that Jesus called his disciples after these events at Nazareth, we know that he must have already had some disciples when these events took place. This conclusion is easily drawn given that his disciples were present when he turned water into wine (John 2:12) which, being the first 'sign' he performed, must have been before those referred to in Luke 4:23

4   I know that this is a little sad... but I like doing sums. If there were six stone jars each holding between twenty to thirty gallons, it would be fair to estimate an average of twenty-five gallons per jar. If this was the case, then Jesus presented the bride and groom with the equivalent of three average wheely-bins of wine. That sounds like some party!

5   Matthew 18:20

6   Some historians believe that this was a latter development

7   Isaiah 8:3

8   Isaiah 1:1; 8:3

9   A collection of Jewish writings

10 When looking at Isaiah it appears almost impossible to separate the man from his message. In fact such was the harmony between them that Isaiah's eldest son was even called Shear-jashub, meaning 'a remnant will return', Isaiah 7:3

11 Isaiah 45:1

12 Isaiah 61:1

13 Moberly R.W.L, *Old Testament Theology* (Baker Academic 2013) 146

14 It is often pointed out that the chapters of Isaiah mirrors the books of the Bible. The first 39 chapters, mirroring the Old Testament, begin with the sin of the people and the consequences of their rebellion. Chapters 40–66, which mirror the New Testament, start with the amazing statement 'Clear the way through the wilderness for the LORD! Make a straight highway through the wasteland for our God!' (Isaiah 40:3) These words are quoted at the beginning of Mark's gospel and are attributed to the ministry of Jesus' cousin, John. Isaiah then concludes, like the book of Revelation, with a glorious vision of the New Heaven and New Earth. Although it is of course impossible to know whether this framework was intended by God, it is however a great way to remember the basic outline of the book.

15 A couple of centuries before Jesus was born, the Hebrew Old Testament was translated into Greek. This became known as the Septuagint because tradition held it was translated by seventy scholars over seventy days. It is now referred to in theology with the letters LXX (meaning seventy).

16 This may also be taken from Isaiah 42:7 which speaks of the Messiah

17 For example Luke 3:3; 24:47; Acts 2:38

CHAPTER TWO: FIRM FOUNDATIONS

18 Christopher J.H. Wright, *The Mission of God* (Inter-Varsity Press, 2011), 21

19 Genesis 1:27

20 John 1:14

21 Exodus 3:14

22 Daniel 7:13; 8:17

23 John 10:36; 20:31

24 Luke 1:35; Matthew 4:3; 14:33; Mark 3:11; John 1:49; Matthew 16:16; 26:63; 27:54; John 20:31; Acts 9:20

25 John 1:12; Romans 8:14; Galatians 3:26; 1 John 1:12

26 Including Matthew 2:5–10; 10:18; John 5:23; 20:28; Romans 9:5; Colossians 1:15–20; 2:9; Titus 2:13; Hebrews 1:8 and 1 John 5:20

27 This *emptying* is sometimes described as Jesus 'laid aside his divinity'. However this unclear terminology is open to misunderstanding. We need to be clear that Jesus did not abandon his divine attributes (since then he would only be a man), but they simply became latent in him. A better expression would be to say that Jesus 'veiled his divinity'. As Gerald F. Hawthorne argues, *The Presence and The Power*, (Wipf and Stock Publishers, 1991)207 that Philippians 2:7 'indicates quite emphatically, although paradoxically, that Christ's self-giving was accomplished by taking, that his self-emptying was achieved by becoming what he was not before, that his kenosis came about not by subtraction but by addition, that his kenosis (an emptying) a filling.'
As we explore this subject, I believe we need to avoid the two equal and opposite errors of (1) pursuing God's Spirit while failing to honour orthodox theology and (2) defending orthodox theology while failing to pursue God's Spirit. For a more substantial discussion on the 'Kenosis Theory' see Wayne Grudem, *Systematic Theology* (Inter-Varsity Press, 2012) 549

28 It should be noted that Scripture is silent on whether Jesus was ever sick. The fact, however, that he suffered pain on the cross is indisputable.

29 Wayne Grudem,539

30 Psalm 90:2; Habakuk 1:13; James 1:17; Revelation 1:8

31 Sam Storms www.samstorms.com/all-articles/post/ could-jesus-have-sinned--2-cor--5:21-

32 Millard J. Erickson, *Systematic Theology* (Baker Books, 2004) 738

NO PLAN B

CHAPTER THREE: THE ANOINTED ONE

33 I have recently discovered a brilliant book: Gerald F. Hawthorne, *The Presence and The Power*, (Wipf & Stock Publishers, 2003) which explores this subject thoroughly. I am also grateful to Dr Sam Storms who helpfully spoke on this subject at the Life in the Spirit conference a number of years ago.

34 Luke 1:46–55

35 Matthew 3:14

36 Exodus 29:4

37 Mark 1:9–11

38 www.samstorms.com/all-articles/post/kenotic-view

39 Genesis 1:2; 8:11; Leviticus 12:8

40 Galatians 5:1

41 Douglas MacMillan, *Jesus. Power without Measure* (Bryntirion Press, 2016) 108

42 Note for example Psalm 8:1 where David writes, 'O LORD, our LORD, your majestic name fills the earth!'

43 Isaiah 61:1 (See also 11:2; 42:1)

44 www.samstorms.com/all-articles/post/kenotic-view

45 2 Corinthians 12:9

46 Romans 8:11

47 In recent years, a number of popular speakers and writers have used Jesus' example of a man entirely dependent on the Spirit in order to challenge us to see even greater miracles, in fulfilment of John 14:12. I believe that we need to hold this challenge alongside the fact that Jesus was both God and man in one person.

48 If you want to read a wonderful and brief book on this subject, I would highly recommend Michael Reeves, *The Good God* (Paternoster, 2012)

NOTES

CHAPTER FOUR: PREACH

49 Kevin DeYoug & Greg Gilbert, *What is the Mission of the Church?* (Crossway, 2011) 93

50 Tom Wright, *Simply Good News* (SPCK, 2105) 24

51 A helpful discussion concerning different views of the Atonement can be found in Wayne Grudem, *Systematic Theology*, (Inter-Varsity Press, 2012) 568 ff

52 John Piper, *God is the Gospel* (Inter-Varsity Press, 2005) 32

53 Timothy Keller, *Center Church* (Zondervan, 2012) 30

CHAPTER FIVE: THE POOR

54 e.g. Exodus 23:11; Leviticus 19:10; 23:22; 25:35; Deuteronomy 15:7

55 Leviticus 12:6–8

56 Luke 19:1–10

57 John 1:3; Colossians 1:16

58 Luke 23:33

59 Abraham Kuyper, *The Work of the Holy Spirit* (Grand Rapids, Eerdmans, 1956) 107- Quoted by MacMillan 21

60 Luke 6:17–26

61 Matthew 5:3

62 D.A. Carson, *Jesus Sermon on the Mount* (Global Christian Publishers, 1999) 18

63 In the same message Jesus rebukes the wealthy, who have 'already received your comfort' (Luke 6:12). These warnings continue to be repeated. For example in Luke 11:39–41 he accuses those religious leaders, known as the Pharisees, for hypocrisy for their neglect and presumably exploitation of the poor.

64 Luke 14:15–24

65 Luke 21:1–4

66 Luke 16:19–31

67 On this note I am incredibly grateful to ministries such as The Message and Christians Against Poverty. These faith-led organisations continue to proclaim the gospel faithfully and serve the world practically. In doing so, I believe they become models for the church. I trust and pray that God will continue to raise up many more like them.

68 Martin Charlesworth and Natalie Williams, *A Church for the Poor* (David C Cook, 2017), 34–46

69 Luke 10:27

70 Ronald J. Sider, *Good News and Good Works* (Baker Books, 2007), 138

71 Luke 19:11–27

72 Ephesians 2:14

73 Frank Houghton (1894–1972)

CHAPTER SIX: PRISONERS

74 Although focusing on Luke's account, we will also reference both Matthew 9:18–26 and Mark 5:22–43

75 William Hendriksen, *Luke* (Banner of Truth Trust, 1979) 456–7

76 Darrell Bock, 159

77 Numbers 15:37–41; Deuteronomy 22:12

78 Matthew 14:36; Mark 6:56

79 Luke 5:12–13

80 Matthew 17:20

81 1 Corinthians 13:12

82 See also John 8:28; 12:49

83 2 Corinthians 11: 23–28

84 Aaron Keyes, *Sovereign over us*, 2011

NOTES

CHAPTER SEVEN: BLIND SIGHT

85 John Wimber, *Power Evangelism* (Hodder and Stoughton, 1985) 101

86 Many no doubt thought that this was highly appropriate, believing blindness to be caused by sin. See John 9:2

87 Isaiah prophesied the Messiah would open blind eyes in Isaiah 35:5–6, 42:6–7. Although Isaiah 61:1–2 does not include the Messiah restoring the sight of the blind, the statement is included in the Septuagint (the Greek translation of the Hebrew Old Testament). Additionally Jesus includes it when sharing his Messianic credentials to a delegation from John (Luke 7:20–22). Out of around twenty-five specific healings of Jesus, recorded in the four gospels, it is the healing of the blind that is reported most.

88 Douglas MacMillan, 138

89 Luke 3:22

90 John 11:1–10

91 Mark 6:5

92 Luke 8:40–56

93 See also Jesus' words concerning the Spirit, John 16:13

94 John 1:3

95 John 3:34

96 Luke 9:1–6; Luke 10:1–10

97 Alan Scott, *Scattered Servants* (David C Cook, 2018) 119

98 The Greek speaks about Gifts of Healings, suggesting that different gifts are given in order to accomplish different healings. The inference is that nobody is fully-equipped with the Gift of Healing period!

99 It is vital to realise that all of God's blessings (spiritual and physical) come through the finished work of Christ on the cross (the atonement) applied by the power of the Spirit. The question is whether physical blessings (such as healing) are, as some claim, the present assured right of the believer in the same way as forgiveness of sins is. I do not hold this view for a number of reasons: (1) it is based on a wrong application of Isaiah 53:4-5 in Matthew 8:17 and 1 Peter 2:24 which have spiritual

rather than physical healing in view; (2) there are numerous of examples of sickness within the New Testament church and Apostolic teaching; (3) it ignores a biblical theology of suffering; (4) it produces a pastoral minefield in in which a lack of healing undermines faith. (With thanks to Peter H. Lawrence, The Spirit who Heals (Kingsway Publications, 2006))

However, I acknowledge that many of those with whom I disagree over the extent of healing in the atonement have healing ministries that far exceed mine. I therefore honour their faith and example, allowing them to challenge the need for me to witness more physical healing in my own ministry.

CHAPTER EIGHT: OPPRESSED

100 Although it has been suggested that this statement was added either by Luke or by a subsequent editor, this appears to undermine the integrity of the text

101 For those who want to explore this subject further, I would wholeheartedly recommend: David Devenish, Demolishing Strongholds (Authentic Lifestyle, 2003); D. Martyn Lloyd-Jones, The Christian Warfare; Arthur Neil, Aid us in our Strife, Volume 1 & 2 (Out of print, but available from second-hand booksellers)

102 John 1:1–3; Colossians 1:16

103 Job 1:6–12

104 Isaiah 14:12–15; Ezekiel 20:12–19; Revelation 12:7–9

105 Hebrews 2:14; 1 John 3:8

106 Daniel 10; Revelation 12

107 2 Corinthians 4:4; Ephesians 6; Colossians 1:12–13; 1 John 5:!9

108 www.samstorms.com/all-articles/post/demons

109 Matthew 4:24; 8:16, 28, 33; 9:32; 12:22; 15:22; Mark 1:32; 5:15, 16, 18, 26; Luke 8:36; John 10:21

110 Matthew 11:18; Mark 3:30; 5:15; 7:25; 9:17; Luke 4:33; 7:33; 8:27; John 7:20; 8:48; 49; 52; 10:20; Acts 8:7; 16:16; 19:13 (See also someone 'with a demon' Mark 1:23; 5:2)

NOTES

https://www.samstorms.com/all-articles/post/nature-of-demonization

111 Luke 9:28–36

112 In terms of good pastoral practice, I would advise starting to pray into physical manifestations without assuming a spiritual root. However, being aware that demons do not always *make themselves known*, ask that the Spirit would reveal any strongholds as you continue to minister.

113 Exodus 7:5; 8:19; 10:7; 31:18; Psalm 8:3

114 Exodus 8:19

Craig A. Evans, *New International Bible Commentary, Luke* (Hendrickson Publishers, 2002) 186

115 Although in recent years much has been written on territorial spirits, I have found David Devenish, *Demolishing Strongholds*, most helpful.

116 Note the warning that Jesus issues at the end of this story. Those who are released from demonic influence must fill the void with God's presence, otherwise the demon will return with a host of others!

117 C.S. Lewis, *The Screwtape Letters* (Harper Collins, 1996 (orig 1942)) ix

118 1 Chronicles 21:1; Acts 5:3

119 Acts 13:6–10

120 Ephesians 6:14–17

121 Different Greek words are used for the 'word' in relation to the sword of the Spirit. Here it is *rhema* and in Heb 4:12 it is *logos*. Although some see them as synonymous, it is possible that *rhema* has a specific emphasis on the application of Scripture (or a prophetic insight) by the Spirit as a word of God applied to a present specific situation rather than the broader principles of biblical truth for all time suggested by *logos*. It is worth noting that the term 'sword' is used in conjunction with this word (the *rhema*) as well as the word (the *logos*) in Hebrews 4:12. It is possible then to refer to both Scripture and prophecy as the 'Sword of the Spirit'.

122 I. Howard Marshall, *The New International Greek Testament Commentary, The Gospel of Luke* (Paternoster Press Ltd, 1998) 428

123 Derek Tidball, *The Reality of Christ – Colossians for Today* (Christian Focus Publications, 1999) 101

CHAPTER NINE: JUBILEE

124 A.J. Jacobs, *The Year of Living Biblically* (Arrow Books, 2009)

125 J. Alec Motyer, *Isaiah, Tyndale Old Testament Commentaries* (Inter-Varsity Press, 1999) 426

126 This is universally accepted by Old and New Testament commentators

127 See also Nehemiah 10:31

128 Due to the nature of the ways in which the Jewish people counted the years, there is some debate as to whether this was in essence a special Sabbath or an *additional* Sabbath.

129 Despite not being part of the legislation concerning Jubilee, if Jubilee was a special Sabbath it would have incorporated the relief of debts. If however Jubilee was an additional Sabbath, given that debts were cancelled at the end of the Sabbath year (Deuteronomy 15:1), it could be seen as one and the same event.

130 Some translations suggest *excessive interest*

131 In reality this was a form of bonded labour. However God ensured that there were numerous instructions in the Mosaic Law concerning the conduct of masters and the rights of slaves.

132 Leviticus 19:19

133 Leviticus 11:7

134 The Greek word is *paidagógos*, although in our society we may refer to a pedagogue

135 Acts 9:1–9

136 In light of this, Paul rebukes those teachers who suggest Gentiles who want to become Christians must first be circumcised. Paul suggests that these teachers should not be satisfied with their own circumcision but 'go the whole way and emasculate themselves' (Galatians 5:12). Ouch!

137 See also Luke 24:27

138 Matthew 5:17

139 Luke 13:10–17

140 Luke 22:7

141 1 John 2:2

142 I am aware that there is a range of views about how the law applies to
Christians. These range from those who argue that a Christian has no
relationship with the law (antinomianism) to religious legalism. I would
want to avoid these extremes.
For further information see, Christopher Bennett; http://www.affinity.
org.uk/downloads/foundations/Foundations%20Archive/43_32.pdf
Richard Hays https://biblicalstudies.org.uk/article_law_hays.html

143 J. Nolland Luke 1–9:20, *Word Biblical Commentary* (Word Books,
1989) 197

144 2 Corinthians 5:21

145 Luke 9:23

CHAPTER TEN: THE TWIST IN THE TALE

146 As far as we know, women were never crucified by the Roman
authorities.

147 Matthew 7:13–14

148 1 Corinthians 1:24

149 1 Peter 3:15

150 Darrell L. Bock, *Luke* (Inter-Varsity Press, 1994) 162

151 2 Timothy 3:16

152 B Webb, *The Message of Isaiah, The Bible Speaks Today* (Inter-Varsity
Press, 1996) 233

APPENDIX

153 For those who want to explore these themes more thoroughly I would
highly recommend Jack Deere, *Surprised by the Power of the Holy
Spirit* (Kingsway Publications, 1993). Through brilliant scholarship and
personal experience, Deere 'debunks' the argument of cessationism. See

also R.T. Kendal, *Holy Fire* (Charisma House, 2014); Simon Ponsonby, *More* (Victor, 2004); Lee Strobel, *The Case for Miracles* (Zondervan, 2018); Andrew Wilson, *Spirit and Sacrament* (Zondervan, 2019)

ACKNOWLEDGEMENTS

I would like to thank those people without whom this book would not be possible.

Firstly, a big thanks to Andy Hawthorne for agreeing to publish before I had put pen to paper. Appreciation also to Ian Rowbottom and the wider team for ensuring it happened. We remain thankful for our many friends at the Message and continue to cheer you on from a distance!

I am deeply grateful to the Kinetic Network team for your ongoing support and encouragement. I trust our partnership in the gospel will remain for years to come. Thank you especially to Will Loescher and Roger Welch for working through my draft, highlighting flaws and suggesting changes. Although faults may remain, they are substantially less, thanks to your diligence.

I remain ever grateful to the trustees, elders and the wider team at Ridgeway Community Church. Thank you for providing me with 'writing time' and for covering in my absence. Thank you also to both congregations, Didcot and Wallingford, for your continued prayer and encouragement.

Lastly, to my wonderful wife Tracey. I am forever grateful for your fun, friendship and patience!

KINETIC NETWORK

Gareth is privileged to lead Kinetic Network, a relational network of leaders and churches committed to the transformation of individuals, churches, society and nations through the Spirit and the Word.

Kinetic Network host the annual Life in the Spirit conference and NGI (Next Generation Impartation) Training Programme. For more information see **www.kineticnetwork.org**

NGI

The aim of NGI (Next Generation Impartation) is to support, encourage and develop young men and women in the values of Transformation by the Spirit and the Word.

NGI is a one- or two-year programme involving:

- Placement in a local church
- Three central study weeks
- Attendance at our annual Life in the Spirit Conference
- 12 hours of weekly guided study in the areas of Bible, Theology, History, Character Formation, Personal Calling & Giftings, Leadership, Ministry, God's Presence, and Mission/Society
- Support from a NGI facilitator and local mentor
- Personalised approach for your specific abilities, learning style, calling, and gifts

NGI is intentionally affordable and is accredited by Moorlands College.

To find out more contact Will Loescher (Course Director) on **willieloe@btinternet.com** or apply online at **www.kineticnetwork.org**